THE LONG BEACH PENINSULA
WHERE THE COLUMBIA MEETS THE PACIFIC

Fort Columbia soldiers with a U.S. Army wagon and mules in 1895. Washington State Parks and Recreation Commission.

THE MAKING OF AMERICA

THE LONG BEACH PENINSULA

WHERE THE COLUMBIA MEETS THE PACIFIC

DONELLA J. LUCERO AND NANCY L. HOBBS

ARCADIA
PUBLISHING

Published by Arcadia Publishing,
Charleston SC, Chicago IL, Portsmouth NH, San Francisco CA

Printed in the United States

Library of Congress control number: 2003113553

For all general information contact Arcadia Publishing at:
Telephone 843-853-2070
Fax 843-853-0044
E-Mail sales@arcadiapublishing.com
For customer service and orders:
Toll-Free 1-888-313-2665

Visit us on the Internet at www.arcadiapublishing.com

CONTENTS

ACKNOWLEDGMENTS

To write a book on the Long Beach Peninsula and its unique communities has been an interesting and challenging task. We relied on many different resources for both information and photographs. Many times we came across inaccurate or conflicting information, and in those cases we made every attempt to sort out the conflicts.

Both of us were born in Ilwaco and lived in Long Beach for much of our childhood and teen years. Donella now lives on the Peninsula, in Ocean Park, and Nancy lives in Spokane, Washington, and has a summer home in Long Beach. Many of the stories and much of the history of the Long Beach Peninsula we remember being told to us by our grandparents and parents, who also called the Peninsula their home. To verify the information in the book, much research took place. We have made every attempt to corroborate our information through knowledgeable people and other sources. It is those people who made this all possible, and who we would like to acknowledge and thank.

We must first acknowledge our husbands, Jim Hobbs and Don Lucero. Their incredible encouragement and support throughout helped us to complete this book. Their help with comments, ideas, and editing was tremendous.

We give love and gratitude to our father, Don Urban, who gave us the passion of history as we grew up. We thank him for the stories and history he gave us about the Long Beach Peninsula, as well as some of the photographs we were able to share with our readers.

We give a special thanks and acknowledgement to Dick and Martha Murfin. We appreciate the opportunity to share some of your photographs.

Lolita Morris, daughter of Gilbert and Lottie Tinker, has been a lifelong friend. She has shared many incidences of her life with us, which we relayed in this book. Thank you Lolita.

Acknowledgments

We want to acknowledge Ryan Karlson, who helped answer many of our questions related to military and marine sites. His help with some of the historical aspects of this book was priceless.

We give a special thanks to Melody Chesnut, who helped us with some of the editing. Thanks Melody.

We also acknowledge and thank the staff of Washington State Parks and Recreation Commission, Lewis and Clark Interpretive Center, University of Washington Archives, Willapa Bay Interpretive Center, Washington State Department of Fisheries and Wildlife, Washington State Extension Services, Cranberry Research Office, Timberland Regional Library, Ocean Park branch, and the Ilwaco Heritage Museum.

We thank all of you for helping in our quest for information and in our search for interesting and informative photographs. Without your assistance we would not have achieved our goal of providing this historical perspective of the Long Beach Peninsula, its communities, and resources.

The Long Beach Peninsula is home to us. The people are friendly, the pace is slow, and the atmosphere spectacular. During the year, crowds converge on this area. With the crowds come some of the festivals and events that celebrate the heritage and resources of the area. We hope this book suitably reflects our love for this area, its history, and people.

INTRODUCTION

The Long Beach Peninsula is located in the far southwestern corner of the state of Washington in Pacific County. Attached to the mainland by a slender three-mile stretch, it is bordered by the Columbia River to the south, the Pacific Ocean to the west, and to the north and east by Willapa Bay. The peninsula is 32 miles long and approximately two and a half miles wide and is best known for its 28-mile driving beach, razor clams, fishing, oysters, and cranberries, and as a major tourist destination.

During the early days when visitors first came to enjoy the beach and relax, the peninsula was known as the North Beach Peninsula, and Willapa Bay as Shoalwater Bay. Tourists traveled to the beach via ferries from Portland and Astoria. Boats, trains, and stages were used in the late nineteenth century and early twentieth century to allow visitors to travel to and along the peninsula. There are no longer ferries or horse-drawn stages to make the slow leisurely trip to the coast; visitors now arrive in a short time by car. The driving time from Seattle and Portland is approximately three to four hours.

The Long Beach Peninsula is full of interesting history with many opportunities to learn and experience the past through the museums and interpretive centers located here. You can visually experience the beauty and wildlife of the area by visiting the parks, lighthouses, forts, ocean beach, river, and bay.

The peninsula is the land of the Chinook Indians, the end of the trail for the Lewis and Clark expedition, and a visiting destination for tourists. The seven main communities located here include Oysterville, Nahcotta, Ocean Park, Long Beach, Seaview, Ilwaco, and Chinook. Only Long Beach and Ilwaco are incorporated towns. On the peninsula map you can see the locations of the communities and other areas of interest discussed in the following chapters.

This book provides the reader with an overview of the history of the Long Beach Peninsula from Native-American settlement to the present day. Chapter

Introduction

one highlights Native-American settlement and exploration prior to 1880. The first settlers, the Chinook Indians, were living on the peninsula when seafarers, traders, and explorers such as Robert Gray, John Meares, Bruno do Heceta, and Lewis and Clark came to the area. In chapter two, the founding and settlement of communities such as Chinook/Chinookville, Pacific City, Ilwaco, Seaview, Long Beach, Klipsan Beach, Ocean Park, Nahcotta/Sealand, and Oysterville are discussed. Chapter three examines the maritime and military presence including forts, lighthouses, lightships, and the jetties. The presence of the U.S. Army, Life Saving Service, and the United States Coast Guard on the peninsula will also be looked at. The early development of the peninsula including transportation is found in chapter four. This chapter includes a discussion of boats, trains, and stages as a means to travel to and on the peninsula. Natural resources–based industries such as commercial clamming, oystering, fishing, logging, and cranberry growing in the area are highlighted in chapter five. These industries, along with tourism, are major contributors to the economics of the peninsula. Chapter six looks at the Long Beach Peninsula as an early tourist destination including a view of early shipwrecks, tourist attractions, activities, and festivals. The last chapter, chapter seven, discusses the present day peninsula, things to see and do, museums, parks, and events. Throughout, the beauty of the Long Beach Peninsula provides a backdrop to the story of how it became the destination it is today.

Chapter One

NATIVE AMERICANS

AND EXPLORATION

The Chinook Indians originally settled the land now known as the Long Beach Peninsula many centuries ago. They continued to thrive in the area long after Robert Gray discovered the Columbia River in 1792 and after Lewis and Clark explored the region in 1805, opening the way for European settlement.

The Chinook were the first people to utilize the abundance of wildlife, fish, and edible plants on the peninsula and the surrounding area. There were deer, elk, fish, shellfish, several types of berries, and roots available to the native people. They caught salmon with nets and spears and taught many of the early settlers their methods of fishing. The strategic position of the Chinook tribe on the lower Columbia River established them as traders with both inland and coastal tribes long before the arrival of Europeans. Because of this, arriving traders and settlers combined the Chinook language with French and English and were able to use this "Chinook jargon" to effectively communicate with many other tribes in the Northwest. Though greatly affected by the new diseases brought by outside settlers and the taking of their land and resources, the descendants of the original Chinook still maintain their tribal culture and continue to live on the peninsula today.

According to a native legend, before the Long Beach Peninsula existed, many warriors in a large canoe paddled along the ocean to the river we now know as the Columbia. The warriors attempted to paddle up the river but the wind continually blew them back. When they could not continue paddling against the wind, they tied their canoe to the rocks and walked upriver to the main Chinook village. The natives visited with the people of the village and returned after many days to where they had tied their vessel. They searched for their canoe but were unable to find it. Where it had been, a large narrow finger of land partially surrounded by water had appeared. The ocean was to the west of the land and a large bay appeared on the north and east. The natives built their houses on this land and lived off the fish, oysters, clams, crabs, and cranberries they found there. This is one version of the legend of how the Long Beach Peninsula was formed.

The mouth of a great river in this region was first noted in 1570 on a map of the world in the *Theatrum Orbis Terrarum*, developed by the prominent Flemish scholar and geographer Abraham Ortelius. Later explorers used this map in their search for the "Great River of the West." It was rumored that ample wealth could be found in the land accessed by this river and both England and Spain continued to hunt for the western gateway to the "Northwest Passage" as they sailed up and down the coastline.

On August 17, 1775, Bruno de Heceta, on his ship *Santiago*, found what looked like the opening to a river that was noted on one of his charts. Though he thought it might be the outlet of a great river, he was unable to explore it further due to the illness of his crew. Heceta named the great bay Bahia de la Asuncion. He called the cape to the south Frondoso, meaning leafy, and the cape to the north San Roque, after the patron saint of the sick and suffering. We now know that what Heceta found was the mouth of the Columbia River.

Thirteen years later, in 1788, Captain John Meares, on the English ship *Felice*, was looking for what was noted on Heceta's chart as Entrada de Heceta. He tried to find the great river that Heceta thought was there. He sailed around Cape San Roque on July 6, but he did not proceed far enough to see the river. Because of this, Meares decided there was no great river and that the large expanse of water in front of him was just a large bay. In his journal, Meares stated, "We can now, with safety, assert that no such river as that of Saint Roc exists." He renamed San Roque "Cape Disappointment" and his presumed bay "Deception Bay." England was hoping to discover Heceta's large river in order to gain possession of the land through discovery. The custom at the time was when a new river was discovered, all the land drained by the river reverted to the nation responsible for its discovery. It had been Meares's hope that he could claim this territory for England, but he came away discovering only the bay just to the north, which he named Shoalwater. We now know it as Willapa Bay.

The first documented ship to enter the mouth of Meares's Deception Bay was the *Columbia Rediviva*, captained by the American Robert Gray. In 1790, Gray and his ship became the first American crew to sail around the world. Gray had heard of a great river in the Northwest and had noted a strong outgoing current in this location as he passed along the Pacific coast, but there was bad weather at the time and he did not attempt to investigate further. Gray discussed this possible river with Captain George Vancouver, who had concluded like Meares that it was not a river but in fact a large bay. Gray, however, was determined to investigate.

The *Columbia Rediviva* entered the "bay" and crossed the river bar on May 11, 1792. Gray sailed about 15 miles up the river, which was later named for his ship, to a point below today's Point Ellis. Here he found a Chinook village where his crew had the opportunity to trade with the natives. The discovery was long sought by various countries, which all hoped to profit from the furs and other resources, as well as the addition of land to their holdings. Gray's visit laid a claim for the young American nation. Incidentally, Gray also named the capes at the mouth of the river. The cape to the south he called Point Adams and the one to the north, Hancock. While the name Cape Hancock can be found on several maps, most continue to call it Cape Disappointment, the name given to it by John Meares.

After exploring and charting the lower part of the river, Gray turned north and continued his trading expedition up the Pacific coast. When the *Columbia Rediviva* was damaged by a storm, Gray stopped at the settlement of Nootka on Vancouver Island. While in port for repairs, he gave a copy of his chart to Don Juan Francisco de la Bodega y Quadra. Captain Vancouver later saw this chart and in October of 1792 sent Captain William Broughton in the *Chatham* to explore Gray's river. When Broughton entered the river he found the British ship *Jenny* with James Baker as her captain anchored in the bay. This inlet, just off Ilwaco, was named Baker's Bay. Broughton sailed much further into the river than Gray, charting it and the landforms he saw. When he sailed out of again, he followed Baker over the Columbia River bar. Captain Broughton later attempted to claim this river and its territory for England, but was not successful. England eventually acknowledged that Captain Robert Gray had discovered the river and that the rightful claim lay with the United States. Captain James Baker is now credited with being the second to enter the Columbia River.

After its discovery, the Columbia was visited by many ships, which anchored along the river to trade with the natives for furs. Most of the vessels anchored in Baker's Bay, and many anchored near the present Fort Canby.

THE LONG BEACH PENINSULA

September 25, 1795, Captain Bishop and the English ship *Ruby* anchored ᴗ aker's Bay. The ship's log states that the crew killed wild birds near what is now called McKenzie Head and planted the seeds of peas, beans, celery, and radishes on a small island in the bay. The crew was able to reap its harvest on the return voyage. According to the June 24, 1956 *Seattle Sunday Times*, this planting was the "first horticultural enterprise in the Pacific Northwest." In the article, it was reported that vegetable plants were still growing on the island more than 50 years after the original plants were seeded.

Several years later this same area—after being visited for many years by sea—was traversed by Lewis and Clark, who were traveling by land. Their expedition was commissioned by President Thomas Jefferson, who was interested in what lay beyond the Mississippi River even before he became president in 1801. After the United States acquired a large expanse of new territory with the 1803 Louisiana Purchase, Jefferson convinced Congress to appropriate money for an overland expedition to the Pacific Ocean. Captain Meriweather Lewis, Jefferson's secretary, was selected to lead the expedition. Lewis chose as his co-commander his friend Captain William Clark, with whom he had served in the military. The purpose of the expedition was to lay the groundwork for a trade route across the continent. Jefferson wanted the United States to reap the benefits of the fur trade and also to find that important portage between the Columbia and the Missouri, while establishing friendly relations with the Native Americans. Information about the country, its climate, topography, vegetation, animal life, and Indian tribes was very important and Jefferson expected detailed reports on all of these. Lewis and Clark gathered supplies and a crew and began their expedition from St. Louis in 1804.

On November 7, 1805, Lewis and Clark reached the lower Columbia River. They saw a large expanse of water and thought they were viewing the Pacific Ocean for the first time. "Great joy in camp we are in View of the Ocian, this great pacific Octean which we been So long anxious to See," wrote Clark in his journal. The expedition had not yet seen the ocean, but had mistaken an inlet of the Columbia River for the Pacific. They continued west toward the coast but moved very slowly in the rain and storms until they could not go any further.

From November 10 through 15, the expedition as a whole was unable to advance any further toward the Pacific Ocean. They were trapped just to the east of Point Ellis in what Clark referred to as a "dismal nitch." The coastal storms came one after the other, holding them to this wet and miserable place. They were in a depressing situation, everything they owned was wet, and their leather clothing was disintegrating.

On November 13, three members of the expedition attempted to make their way around the point using an Indian canoe. They were successful in making it to the other side and on November 14 one of them came overland to tell Clark what they found: a sandy beach and an Indian village. Lewis took a small party around the point and down the river. While he and some of his men continued on toward the ocean, Clark and the rest of the party came around the point to the beach. The men built a camp with boards taken from deserted Chinook lodges and Clark noted that he could see from this location the ocean from Point Adams to Cape Disappointment. They camped at what is called "Station Camp" near Chinookville. Station Camp served as the expedition's main base and is near where Clark made his measurements of the uncharted country they had crossed.

On November 17, Lewis and his party returned. They had traveled by land up toward Cape Disappointment and north along the beach for several miles before coming back. According to Clark's journal on this day, he "directed all the men who wished to See more of the main Ocian to prepare themselves to Set out with me early on tomorrow morning." The next day Clark went by land with several men to view the Pacific. They walked along Baker's Bay and in the area near the present Fort Canby, Clark and his group found a tree with Lewis's name carved on it. Clark carved his name as well, along with the month and year, and added "by land." He noted in his journal that several of his men also carved their names.

Clark's party crossed toward the ocean and climbed a "bald hill" thought to be what is now known as McKenzie Head. The group camped just north of this location. They continued north through the trees and hills, up the shore to a place near the present town of Long Beach. During his exploration of the area, Clark marked his name on another small pine tree, including the day, month, and year (November 19, 1805). From here they returned to Station Camp. The expedition party continued to explore the area and learned about the natives, plants, and animals until November 25, when they crossed the Columbia River to set up a winter camp before returning home the following spring.

THE LONG BEACH PENINSULA

It was on the Long Beach Peninsula that Lewis and Clark were able to finally stand at the western edge of the continent and fulfill the charge given them by President Jefferson. It was here they completed their long journey to the Pacific Ocean.

Several years later on August 19, 1818, Captain James Biddle of the U.S. Navy anchored his ship *Ontario* at the anchorage site near the present Fort Canby. Biddle had been sent by President James Monroe and Secretary of State John Quincy Adams to take formal possession of this territory for the United States. Biddle went ashore with 50 of his sailors and with due ceremony nailed a lead tablet to a tree. With this act he formally claimed both the north and south shores of the river for the United States. Later in the year, John Prevost arrived at Fort George, now Astoria, and raised the U.S. flag over the fort, reasserting Biddle's claim.

The path was now open for further exploration and settlement of this remote area. Within several decades, American communities took over and the land of the Chinook was changed forever.

Chapter Two

FOUNDING AND SETTLEMENT

Several small communities have been located on the Long Beach Peninsula: Oysterville, Nahcotta/Sealand, Ocean Park, Klipsan Beach, Long Beach, Seaview, Pacific City, Ilwaco, and Chinookville/Chinook. While tied together by location, natural resources, and history, each is also unique in itself. They have all seen both success and failure, but most continue to persevere and turn their individual qualities into a positive force for the future.

As time has passed, these communities have changed. Some have disappeared. Sealand, Pacific City, and Chinookville, for example, are no longer to be seen. But while visitors can't enjoy these towns, their history and their role in developing the Long Beach Peninsula remains.

Oysterville

The town of Oysterville is on the north end of the peninsula on Willapa Bay, formerly known as Shoalwater Bay. Its name came from the oyster industry that helped establish the town.

In the early days, this was the winter home of the Chinook Indians. They called the area tsako-te-hahsh-eetl, or place of the red-topped grass. The Chinook took advantage of the many oysters found in the bay, eating them as food. It was this same abundance of shellfish that brought settlers to the area and eventually led to the formation of the town of Oysterville.

In 1853, Robert Hamilton Espy was working near Chinook as a timber scout. He met Isaac A. Clark, and together they cut timber pilings and scouted the west side of Shoalwater Bay for oysters. Espy and Clark, now considered the founding fathers of Oysterville, had heard through Chinook Chief Nahcati that many oysters could be found on the west side of the bay; that is exactly what they discovered. In 1854, Espy began to buy up oyster grounds on the bay and Clark took out a donation land claim and platted the town of Oysterville. Espy started the Shoalwater Bay Oyster Company in 1865 and through a merger with another company, the Morgan Oyster Company was formed in 1886. By 1900, Espy was one of the largest landowners in the county, owning approximately 4,000 acres on the north end of the peninsula. As the population of the area grew, his friend Isaac Clark divided his land into lots and sold them to people eager to live near the prosperous oyster beds.

In 1865, a special election was held to vote on the location of the Pacific County seat. The outcome transferred the seat of government from Chinookville on the Columbia River to the more populous Oysterville. By then, the Long Beach Peninsula was part of the Washington Territory. In 1869, a two-story county courthouse was built to house the records and and the court itself. The building had two offices on the ground floor and a courtroom on the upper floor. A jail, located in a separate building, was added to the site about the same time. It contained a steel cell with a wood stove and cooking utensils for the prisoners' use. Years later, after the Oysterville jail was closed for official business, it was used as a barn and storage space until it eventually collapsed.

As the population increased, John and Thomas Crellin made Oysterville their home and started a store and post office in 1856. At first, the mail was brought overland from Chinookville by foot and horseback on old Indian trails and along the beach. In about 1858, Lewis Loomis acquired the mail contract and decided to combine mail service with passenger service. In 1875, he and his partners had a side-wheeler ship built named the *General Canby*, which not only transported mail to the peninsula, but also carried passengers from Astoria, Oregon, across the Columbia to Ilwaco. From there, both mail and passengers were transported by stagecoach. They traveled by way of the beach, then across land to Oysterville. After the railroad was built, the mail came north by rail to Nahcotta where it transferred to a stage to continue on to Oysterville. In 1858, Isaac Clark was appointed postmaster and operated the post office from his general store. Eventually the post office was transferred to the Oysterville Store where it remains today.

In the 1870s, Oysterville was already starting to develop into a tourist destination and the population began to grow even more. By the middle of the decade the town had a population of 500 and enjoyed the services of two hotels, a boat works, blacksmith shop, butcher shop, two barbershops, a tannery, three saloons, and four general stores.

With the increase in population came more children and by 1860 the town felt a school was needed. Classes were held in a number of locations until 1863, when the first school in Pacific County was built in Oysterville. The entire town worked to build the one-room schoolhouse out of redwood delivered by an oyster schooner from San Francisco. This building served the town's needs until 1874, when a larger, two-story schoolhouse was erected to accommodate the growing number of students. This new school unfortunately burned to the ground in 1905 and was not replaced until 1907, when its successor—the schoolhouse still standing in Oysterville today—was built. When this newer, smaller school became overcrowded it was used only for the upper grades with the lower grades attending class in the Winslow Store Building.

The first hotel in Oysterville was the Stevens Hotel, constructed in 1860 to house oyster workers. In 1873 the Pacific Hotel was built and was the largest hotel in the county at the time. It was especially busy when the courts were in session, used often by attorneys traveling from as far away as Portland to try their cases.

The first Methodist church in southwest Washington was built in Oysterville in 1872. The lumber was donated and brought from South Bend, Washington, in an oyster sloop, or plunger. The church blew down in a 1921 storm, leaving the Baptist church, which was built in 1892 and donated by R.H. Espy, as the only remaining church in Oysterville.

On July 19, 1888, the Ilwaco Railroad & Navigation Company arrived in Nahcotta/Sealand. Tourists and locals alike were now able to easily travel from one end of the peninsula to the other. With the arrival of better transportation between the bay and the rest of the peninsula, many visitors decided to spend their summers closer to the beach rather than in Oysterville. This decrease in tourism, along with the failing oyster industry, caused the town's population to begin to decline.

By the 1890s, Oysterville faced competition from South Bend and Nahcotta/Sealand, both of which had ambitions to become the new seat of county government. Nahcotta/Sealand was promoted by the railroad because it was at the end of the rail line. South Bend's citizens called for a ballot to determine the new location, and in the election of 1892 South Bend was apparently voted the new county seat. The people of Oysterville objected to the election, citing that officials allowed non-residents and non-registered voters to participate. Oysterville succeeded in getting a stop order by the court in order to look into the legality of the election, but the officials of South Bend did not honor the order and on Sunday, February 5, 1893, the county records were forcefully removed from Oysterville to South Bend. The story holds that 85 men came from South Bend on two steamers. Several of the men kicked down the door, stormed into the courthouse, and began to remove both the official records and the furniture. County Auditor Phil D. Barney, who was in the building at the time, refused to give up the records in his possession. It was said that Barney put up a good fight and hit several South Benders over the head with a chair leg, but he was outnumbered and despite his protests the group from South Bend stole everything except what was locked in the vault. It was later found by the courts that the election was in fact illegal, but by then it was too late to reverse what had happened. Since then the Pacific County seat has remained in South Bend.

A.B.L. Gellerman started the Peninsula College around 1895 in the former Oysterville courthouse building, which after the raid was no longer being used for its original purpose. About 40 students registered for the first year at a cost of $30 for the entire school year. For two years the institution served both grade school and high school students, but due to low enrollment it did not last very long. R.H. Espy bought the former courthouse building after the school closed and converted it to a barn and house. On December 30, 1940, the building, already in an advanced state of disrepair, collapsed during a windstorm.

In 1920 John Heckes and Louis Kemmer bought another Oysterville landmark, the John Crellin house, to use as a vacation home when they visited the peninsula. It later became a boarding house and restaurant called Heckes House, where one could find good lodging and meals for $10 per week. The house has since reverted to a private home and still stands in Oysterville.

The loss of the courthouse, the lack of a railroad, and the depletion of the oyster beds caused many people to leave Oysterville. Today it is a historic and sleepy little town that still maintains an important oyster industry. It is on the National Register of Historic Places and draws visitors with its many historic homes, views of beautiful Willapa Bay, and plentiful opportunities to purchase its oysters.

Nahcotta/Sealand

Nahcotta is just south of Oysterville on Willapa Bay. It was named in the 1880s by early settler John Peter Paul for local Indian chief Nahcati. The town thrived for a while because it was the end of the Ilwaco Railroad & Navigation Co. rail line. People felt that the railroad would bring tourism and business to the area.

Two communities formed around the railroad tracks. In 1889, John Crellin sold his donation land claim to John Peter Paul, who platted his town of Nahcotta on the south side of the tracks. At about the same time, B.A. Seaborg moved a few miles south of Oysterville and platted the town of Sealand on his donation land claim on the north side of the tracks. The competition that developed between the towns was a result of a fight between Lewis Loomis, the railroad, and B.A. Seaborg. Seaborg was one of the original investors in the Ilwaco Railroad & Navigation Co. and a member of the company's board of directors. As such, he had knowledge of the rail line planned for the peninsula. Because of a misunderstanding between Loomis and Seaborg concerning the property for the railroad's terminus, Seaborg quit the board. However, he knew where the railroad would be built and consequently the best place to put a town to take advantage of it. His town of Sealand was laid out and recorded on February 6, 1889, and included the site of the proposed terminus. Both the railroad and Loomis instead supported the town of Nahcotta in opposition to Seaborg, and as a result of a lawsuit over the issue the railroad received two blocks of Sealand. These blocks would become the location of the railroad terminus at the north end of the peninsula.

The first building to go up in the area was the Sealand Hotel, built by Seaborg. When a petition was made to the government for a post office, one was built in Sealand. Loomis, still angry with Seaborg for taking advantage of his inside knowledge and investing in Sealand, began to help develop the adjoining town of Nahcotta and filed a lawsuit against Seaborg as well. Tiring of the controversy, Seaborg sold his interests and moved back to Ilwaco, where he became quite active in politics.

Meanwhile, in 1890 J.J. Brumbaugh started the *Ilwaco Advance*. Two years later the *Pacific Journal*, which had originally been in Oysterville, moved to Sealand, and then moved again to Ilwaco. The two newspapers took separate sides and continued to highlight and document the continuing fight between Seaborg and Loomis through their editorials.

While the post office and *Pacific Journal* remained in Sealand, and a general store, railroad roundhouse, and shipping facilities were in Nahcotta, the competition remained very much alive until 1893, when the post office was transferred to Nahcotta. After that the surrounding area, including what was once Sealand, became known as Nahcotta.

In 1898, Seaborg leased the Morrison Hotel, formerly the Sealand Hotel, to the innovative Charles Shagren. Shagren built a windmill in order to supply the hotel with hot and cold running water. He remodeled the building and made it into one of the most popular places to stay in the area. That same year Shagren also became postmaster. The hotel's name was eventually changed to the Bayview Hotel.

On the other side of the tracks in 1890, Albert Hughes and his wife built the Nahcotta Hotel. Getting their start in the hospitality industry years before keeping boarders in a tent before the completion of the railroad, the Hughes built up their business and eventually owned one of the most popular hotels in the area.

Morehead and Co., a general store, began in Oysterville in 1885 and moved to Nahcotta upon completion of the railroad. The earliest mercantile on the peninsula, it was owned by both L.A. Loomis and J.A. Morehead and served customers in South Bend and throughout the Long Beach Peninsula. In 1895, due to increase in business, Loomis and Morehead opened another store in Ocean Park. By 1900, Nahcotta had two general stores, the Bayview and Nahcotta Hotels, a high school, a boat works, a train depot, and an Ilwaco railroad machine shop.

A steamer from South Bend and a stage from Oysterville both met the train daily in Nahcotta. Boats also came in several times a week from Nemah and Naselle, and opportunities to travel on and off the Long Beach Peninsula increased. With the variety of boat and train connections, tourists and locals could now travel to outside destinations via public transportation.

Nahcotta was selected as the ending point for the railroad because of its location and the deep channel running from its to the bay entrance. This was the perfect spot for shipping oysters and logs from the bay area via the railroad all the way to the Columbia River. The rail line did not continue as far as Oysterville due to a lack of money and support, but stage and wagon service was available between Oysterville and Nahcotta for those who wished to connect with the train.

On January 15, 1915, a fire started at the Nahcotta Hotel. The flames, carried by the wind, quickly engulfed several nearby businesses including Morehead's General Store, the train depot, and the telephone office. Firefighters came from as far away as Chinook by train to put out the fire, but by the time they got to Nahcotta, much of the core of the town was destroyed. A few buildings were rebuilt after the fire, but the town was never the same.

While Nahcotta did not retain its business district, by 1943 it was the center of the oyster industry. At this time there were six oyster-packing plants, which employed many locals and brought in $2 million annually. Today Nahcotta is still the center of the oyster industry on the peninsula, with an active port facility.

Ocean Park

Due west of Nahcotta, Ocean Park is nine miles north of Long Beach on the coastal side of the peninsula.

The Methodist Church played a major part in the founding of the town. In 1883, Isaac Clark approached both the local Methodists and the Methodists who spent their summers on the peninsula. At the time, they were looking for a location for a church camp away from saloons and "undesirables." Clark's suggestion was for them to hold their camp meetings in an area that would be set aside as a resort. The group incorporated as the Ocean Park Camp Meeting Association of the Methodist Episcopal Church.

Reverend William B. Osborn, who had been the founder of a Methodist camp in Ocean Grove, New Jersey, chose the location: 250 acres between the ocean and the bay. The association platted the ocean side of the site in October of 1883. The plots were 50 feet by 100 feet and were leased only to members for their use. A dirt road and a plank walk joined the camp with Nahcotta and the bay. This walk and road allowed people to go between the ocean and the bay in easy fashion, and as an additional benefit, the children from Ocean Park could walk the plank walkway to school in Nahcotta.

The Taylor Hotel was built in Ocean Park in 1887 to offer visitors a place to stay. W.D. Taylor, a former stage driver for Lewis Loomis, ran the hotel and restaurant with his wife for many years. The old hotel building still stands in Ocean Park and has been used by various businesses over the years.

In 1888, the association began selling plots on the condition that the buyers not use or manufacture alcohol or gamble there. In the beginning members camped in tents, and gradually people began to build cabins out of material found on the beach. With the influx of people, a post office was established in Ocean Park in 1890. Tourism was the town's major industry, with commercial clamming running second. Several clam canneries were built in Ocean Park to process the clams purchased from diggers who worked the coast during low tides.

The founders and early settlers built many wonderful homes in Ocean Park. One of the most unique was built in 1912 and named the "The Wreckage." This home was constructed of logs and drift the owner Guy S. Allison found on the beach. The main house was built with logs that came ashore when a log raft broke loose while coming across the Columbia River bar. A few days after Allison found those logs, another ship, the *President Washington*, lost its propeller and almost went aground near Beard's Hollow. To lighten the load, the crew threw overboard the flooring lumber it was carrying. Allison was able to gather enough of the lumber to construct both decks of his house. The shakes for the roof were made from shingle bolts that washed up on the beach. The house contains six rooms and two porches and was modeled after a blockhouse Allison saw when he traveled to Sitka, Alaska. The Wreckage can still be seen in Ocean Park and is on the National Register of Historic Places.

Ocean Park is a very friendly, small community known as the "home of the clam." For many years the town has been the center of razor clam digging on the peninsula.

Klipsan Beach (Ilwaco Beach)

The second lifesaving station on the peninsula was the Ilwaco Beach station, established in 1889. The first station was built at Cape Disappointment in 1877. The name Ilwaco Beach was later changed to Klipsan Beach, but the station continued to provide lifesaving service for ships and persons in need.

The Ilwaco Beach station was built on property purchased from Edwin Loomis, the brother of Lewis Loomis, who owned the Ilwaco Railroad & Navigation Company. The site provided access to an area of many shipwrecks. From 1889 through 1892, volunteers manned the lifeboats when a ship was in trouble near or on the beach.

On November 3, 1891, when the station was still manned by volunteers, the British ship *Strathblane* struck the beach near the outpost. Though the lifesaving team tried to save the ship's crew, their lines fell short and seven of the *Strathblane's* crew lost their lives, including the captain. The people of the peninsula buried all the victims at the cemetery in Ilwaco. Interestingly, the *Glenmorag*, the sister ship of the *Strathblane*, wrecked five years later just a few miles north.

After the *Strathblane* incident, a full-time crew was ordered for Ilwaco Beach Life Saving Station. In 1892, it consisted of seven surf men and a keeper of the station. Surf men were required to be experienced and able swimmers, under the age of 45, and able to read and write. The keeper was responsible for administrative duties and making sure that all rules and regulations of the U.S. Life Saving Service were followed. He was also responsible for maintaining equipment and training the crew.

Klipsan Beach was primarily a train stop and lifesaving station. A few summer homes were built in the area, but it did not become a self-sustaining community in itself. Ocean Park was the closest town to Klipsan.

Long Beach

Henry Harrison Tinker purchased a land claim from Charles E. Reed in 1880. Shortly after he bought the land—which was little more than a wilderness at the time—Tinker, his wife Nancy, and children Lena, Gilbert, and Harry moved on to the property. Tinker's land was approximately one mile square, where he hoped to build a town and sell property to people wanting to move to the area. Over a period of many years he filled and cleared the land by hand, so others might move in and build up the town. Tinker was guided by a vision of his land with streets, alleys, and many homes. He platted his town and named it Tinkerville. Later, the name was changed to Long Beach.

THE LONG BEACH PENINSULA

Tinkerville became a summer destination for people from Portland, who could buy lots, set up a tent, and enjoy the beach during the summer months. A group of 26 residents from the east side of Portland purchased five acres from Henry Tinker. This group formed the East Portland Camp. Tinker also set aside a tract known as "the Meadows" for the public. He hoped it would eventually become a recreational area within town.

Henry Tinker also built the Long Beach Hotel. When it burned in 1894, he constructed a new one within the next two years. The hotel was located only 10 feet from the railroad tracks in the center of town, as were most of the businesses. It was said that it was so close to the tracks that on rainy days a plank was set down from the coach to the steps of the hotel, which allowed passengers to depart the train without getting their feet wet. The Long Beach Hotel continued to house visitors until it was torn down in 1963 to make way for several new businesses.

There were many wonderful hotels located in or near the town of Long Beach. The Garden Grove Hotel and the Ocean Home were located in an area called Tioga just north of Long Beach. The largest and fanciest was the Breakers Hotel, built in 1901 a bit north of Tioga. Joseph M. Arthur ran the Breakers until it burned down in September 1904. Over the following winter, however, Arthur rebuilt the hotel even bigger than it had been prior to the fire. The new structure was 70 feet by 100 feet and had 126 rooms for guests. It featured a large dining room, and was a modern facility with electricity. It boasted of tennis courts, a bowling alley, and a golf course. It even advertised hot and cold fresh and salt water in every bathtub and claimed of having the "Best Ladies Orchestra and a Large Dancing Pavilion." According to advertisements, the rates were $12 to $18 a week on the American Plan.

Also in Long Beach was the Driftwood Cottage, built in the 1880s by a Mr. Merritt. This hotel was made of logs and driftwood found on the beach. It was purchased by Tom and Mollie Lyniff, who continued adding driftwood, logs, and parts of shipwrecks to the structure. The Driftwood, along with its salt-water bathhouse, was a very popular place to lodge. Staying there in 1910 cost $2 a day.

The Portland Hotel, belonging to the Hanniman family, was built on the north end of Long Beach near the depot. It was a unique hotel in that part of the building had a circular form. The hotel had within it a saloon and dining room for its guests. But on December 6, 1914, the Portland was destroyed by fire and never rebuilt.

Other hotels built in Long Beach had names like Harvest Home, Pacific Hotel, Chamberlin's, Ocean View, and North Beach Inn, many of which were located near the railroad tracks. Closer to the depot near the Long Beach Hotel were seats set out for visitors to wait for the trains. This whole area lining the main portion of town in front of the tracks was called "Rubberneck Row."

North of the main town near the train stops of Tioga and Breakers were the hotels Breakers, Garden Grove, and Ocean Home. To the south of Long Beach near Seaview was another train stop known as Salt Aire. Located at this stop were the cottage-style hotels Sunset Cottage and The Salt Aire. There were many more cottages, boarding houses, small hotels, and even an auto camp in or near Long Beach. During the summer most of them were filled to capacity with summer folk enjoying the beach.

On June 29, 1923, the Shagren Hotel opened in Long Beach. It was advertised as having 16 newly furnished rooms, a dining room, and a lobby. The dining room had an excellent view of the ocean with dinner being served from 5:30 until 7:30. On July 7, 1923, the hotel was to serve a special dinner. For $1, the meal included clear consomme, salmon pattie, combination salad, spring chicken Maryland, new potatoes and peas, sauté corn, fruit jello with whipped cream, and a choice of beverage. The Shagren Hotel, like other hotels on the peninsula, presented great food and clean rooms in order to compete for the already lucrative tourist business.

Even in the early days, the town had many attractions for tourists to enjoy, including curio shops, restaurants, a dance hall, fresh and saltwater baths, and pools. One of the best bathhouses was the Crystal Baths, owned and operated by F.H. Canaris, until it burned down in 1912. Mr. Canaris was a businessman who also owned a curio shop in town. Long Beach tourists were also drawn to the view along the beautiful shoreline, and in the evening bonfires were built with driftwood found on the beach.

Another summer activity, especially for young boys, was a well-known camp in Long Beach called Hill's Summer Camp. It was owned and operated by Joseph and Benjamin Hill, who also ran an academy in Portland for boys aged six to eighteen. This school, called Hill Military Academy, was founded in 1901. In the summers when the academy was closed, the Hills operated their summer camp. It was described in a 1924 advertising brochure as:

> a permanent summer camp, where their cadets and other boys who wish to be entered may spend a wonderful vacation time. A short period in the morning is given over to study, to coaching the boys in the fundamentals or preparing them for high school. The remainder of the day is occupied with play, swimming, picnics—all sorts of pleasures that appeal to the growing boy. Mess time finds all the lads on hand to answer roll call and enjoy the well-prepared meals, which are provided under the direction of an expert chef and capable dietician. A trustworthy housemother and several trained assistants, faculty members and a superintendent regulate and manage every detail of camp life. A little constructive work and considerable play, good meals, regular hours for sleep and exercise, much fresh air, careful discipline, and influences for refinement and wholesome enjoyment round out the camp life at Hill summer camp.

The camp ran from July 1 through September 1 and enrolled about 60 students. It consisted of several buildings including a barracks for housing the boys and staff, a clubhouse, and an administration and dining hall. The buildings were very close to the beach and incorporated the old Black's Hotel that had stood in the same location for many years. The boys got to visit other areas on the peninsula as well, such as Beard's Hollow, the two lighthouses, and the forts. The children fished, rode horses, played sports, and explored. The camp was conducted in a military fashion, but good food, fun, and responsibility were key components of its program.

The Hills sold the camp buildings in 1925. The structure housing the main dining hall and administrative offices was sold to a fraternal organization and renamed Redman Hall. It was just east across the highway from the present Dennis Company. Redman Hall was a popular place for meetings and dances until it was torn down in the late 1970s.

Gilbert Tinker, the son of founder H.H. Tinker, was the first mayor of the newly incorporated Town of Long Beach. He also served on the city council for many years. He and his wife Lottie made visitors feel very welcome to their town. Their daughter Lolita Morris recounted a time she came across her parents standing in the pantry. Gilbert asked Lottie where her old potato masher was. When she asked him why, he said he needed something to get the council's attention and quiet people down during the meetings. Lottie gave him the masher and that is what he used for several years to call the town meetings to order.

Another memory Lolita Morris shared was of her father saying that during one council meeting he went as a friend to all, but upon leaving he had very few friends. This particular meeting was very controversial. Tinker had proposed moving the businesses and buildings back away from the railroad to allow room for cars to drive. At that time the railroad ran down the center of the road and the businesses were only 10 to 15 feet from the tracks. When autos began to be used it became hard to maneuver the vehicles between the train tracks and the businesses. Despite the controversy at the time, the buildings were eventually pulled back, which made it much easier for people to travel around the town.

The Long Beach area and the rest of the peninsula was referred to by Henry David Thoreau in his journal *Excursions on the Sands of Cape Cod in the years 1849, 1850, 1855, & 1857* as compiled and printed in the book *Cape Cod* by Dudley C. Lunt. Thoreau wrote:

> On the Pacific side of our country also no doubt there is good walking to be found; a recent writer and dweller there tells us that "the coast from Cape Disappointment [or the Columbia River] to Cape Flattery [at the Strait of Juan de Fuca] is nearly north and south, and can be traveled almost its entire length on a beautiful sand-beach," with the exception of two bays, four or five rivers, and a few points jutting into the sea.

This entire stretch of beach has for over 100 years been a great playground for beachcombing, picnicking, fishing, clamming, crabbing, surf bathing, and walking. These were many of the same attractions that Henry Tinker saw as drawing cards to his town.

THE LONG BEACH PENINSULA

Seaview

Jonathan L. Stout and his wife Annie received a land grant on June 10, 1873, that would eventually become the resort town of Seaview. His property consisted of 153.5 acres just south of H.H. Tinker's Long Beach site. Stout platted his town in 1881, but he had begun selling parcels of land as early as 1874. He sold lots of 50 feet by 100 feet for as little as $100 per lot to people who wanted to camp or build a cottage at the beach. Several years later in 1886, Stout built the Seaview House, a large hotel that he hoped would attract visitors to the area. Then in 1887, he and Annie divorced. By the terms of the settlement, Annie received the deeds to a significant amount of property on the peninsula.

Jonathan Stout stayed in Seaview after the divorce and continued to build up his resort. He advertised that he was able to pick up guests at the steamship dock in Ilwaco and transport them to his resort. He made sure there was entertainment and a store where his guests could purchase supplies, and he saw to it there were also services available for those who wanted to camp at his Seaview location. He had lots for sale to those who were interested in having a place of their own.

Stout was involved in building the railroad, which he saw as a way to bring more people to both Seaview and the peninsula as a whole. But in 1892, his Seaview House burned to the ground. He never rebuilt, and died three years later.

At the time of his death, Jonathan Stout was in financial difficulty. Much of his property that was not sold for debts went to his daughter Inez, who with her husband Charles Beaver built a home and hotel in Seaview. This became the Shelburne Hotel, which was famous for Inez's wonderful food and was a favorite resort destination for the wealthy of Portland. In 1903, Charles Beaver built a small railroad stop in conjunction with the hotel that became a fine place for the train to drop off or take on passengers.

In 1906, Charles and Inez sold the Shelburne Hotel and property to William C. Hoare. Several years later, Hoare had it moved across the road and turned to face east. The Shelburne continues to operate in this location today.

Frank Strauhal purchased Stout's store and offered to donate a parcel of property to the railroad to build a depot if the line would come through

Seaview. Eventually the train did come through, where it stopped at the new depot and then continued up the peninsula to Nahcotta.

Seaview grew over the years because of people building homes and summer cottages and because of the several businesses that started up near the depot. At one time, there was Strauhal's General Store, a post office, an ice cream store, bakery, meat market, dance hall, and theater. Several other hotels were built in Seaview, including the Gables, Sea Croft, Newton, and Hackney Cottage.

A very popular activity for tourists staying in one of the various Seaview hotels was visiting the "Fishing Rocks" just south of Seaview at Beard's Hollow. Whole families went down to these rocks to spend the day fishing and picnicking. Today Seaview is a small community with a few businesses and many beautiful old homes lining the streets.

Pacific City

On November 15, 1849, Elijah and Sarepta White filed a donation land claim just west of the present town of Ilwaco on Baker's Bay. Here Elijah platted a town and hoped to develop a successful seaport and city at the mouth of the Columbia River. White became a great promoter and salesman, successfully convincing people from the East Coast and other areas to visit, buy his land, invest, and settle at his "Pacific City." He was successful in getting investors to come as well. Some of the first were Edwin G. Loomis, Charles Stewart, and J.D. Holman.

In 1850, Holman purchased a third of White's land claim, then bought a hotel building from the East Coast, which he had disassembled and shipped around Cape Horn. This 60-room hotel, called "The Holman House," was rebuilt on his new property at Pacific City. Loomis and Stewart also purchased property and built the Pacific Steam Mill, a steam sawmill, at the site. The mill, constructed in 1850, was the first steam sawmill in the Washington Territory. Records from this time show that a post office was already in operation at Pacific City. Pacific City was also the first seat of Pacific County, being authorized by the legislature in 1851 when this particular area was still part of the Oregon Territory.

In 1852, J.D. Holman moved to Pacific City where his son Frederick was born. Frederick Holman was said to be the first white child born in the

Washington Territory. An election was recorded at Pacific City the same year, showing 16 people voting in that precinct. Also in 1852 the U.S. Congress set aside more than 600 acres for a military reservation that would later become Fort Canby. This reservation included the majority of land in Pacific City, which was purchased by the government from most of the residents including White, Holman, and Stewart. White continued to own some land that was not included in the military reservation but this property was not near the bay and not a good site for development. By 1865, the post office was no longer in operation and most of the town was deserted. Holman moved to a site just east of Pacific City where he started the town of Unity, later named Ilwaco. Many of the other residents moved to various sites on the peninsula and most of the buildings either burned down or were dismantled for building supplies until no visible signs of Pacific City remained. White, no longer able to realize his dream, moved from the area and died in San Francisco in 1879.

Ilwaco

The town of Ilwaco is located on Baker's Bay on the Columbia River where for generations it was a large settlement of the Chinook Indians. But by the time Lewis and Clark reached the peninsula in 1805, there was no settlement to be seen. When early Europeans came into the area to trade, they brought diseases that killed more than half the tribe. Most of the survivors left for other parts of the peninsula, and new settlers and fishermen coming into the area eventually established the town of Ilwaco where the Chinook had once lived.

The first donation land claim in what is now known as Ilwaco was owned by Columbia River bar pilot Captain James Johnson. Johnson received his claim in 1848 and built a large house there. He lived in Ilwaco with his native wife and children until he drowned while crossing the Columbia. There is a legend that Captain Johnson had buried his money and gold on his property and when he died his wife did not know where it was hidden. Over the years many people have tried to find this treasure, but to date, no one has.

In 1859, Isaac Whealdon purchased Johnson's land from his family and moved into the large house on the hill. Whealdon started a business transporting oysters from Shoalwater Bay to Baker's Bay to waiting ships that would haul them to Astoria. He also set up a freight wagon route utilizing the beach along the Pacific as a natural highway.

Founding and Settlement

The heritage of Ilwaco is closely associated with the history and demise of Pacific City. J.D. Holman, whose property also became a large part of the town of Ilwaco, had been an investor in Elijah White's Pacific City, and many of the Ilwaco settlers had originally come to Pacific City to live and work. After the federal government designated the Pacific City site as part of its 640-acre military and lighthouse reservation in 1852, Holman received a donation land claim east of Pacific City on Baker's Bay. The Union soldiers who were stationed nearby at what became Fort Canby originally called this site Unity. It is said that Ilwaco was named for Elowahka Jim, a native who was married to Elowahka, the daughter of Chinook Chief Comcomally.

Holman made Ilwaco a destination for tourists and settlers. The town site was perfectly located to allow access by ship from Portland and Astoria. Holman had a store, post office, and summer camping facility. He platted the town in 1872 and promoted it and the fishing in Baker's Bay. The settlers in Oregon did not want to see a competing town on the north side of the river, so they spread rumors to potential settlers that there were no fish on the north side and no drifting grounds for nets. It was not until 1882, when fish traps were being set, that Ilwaco began to be settled. People eventually purchased property and built homes there, and the population gradually increased.

Holman and a fisherman named Henry Pike planned the construction of a canal between Shoalwater Bay and Black Lake with a railroad line between the lake and Baker's Bay. This canal and rail line would be used to transport oysters from Shoalwater (Willapa) Bay to ships that would take the valuable shellfish to Astoria. The plan fell apart however when Holman died in 1882.

Fishing was the primary industry of Ilwaco, but farming, logging, and tourism also brought people and businesses to town. Ilwaco merchants also supplied Fort Canby and the Cape Disappointment Life Saving Station with supplies and food.

In 1880, B.A. Seaborg built the Aberdeen Packing Company, a salmon cannery on Baker's Bay in Ilwaco. Seaborg's cannery caught on fire and burned to the ground on August 16, 1898. Most of the people moving to Ilwaco at the time were from Finland, and the Finnish people primarily worked in the cannery or the fishing industry. In 1882, a second cannery, the Cape Hancock Packing Company, was built. Seaborg also owned a sawmill on the north end of Black Lake where boards were cut to make boxes to hold the canned salmon for shipping and for other uses.

Seaborg also owned a general store and was active in Ilwaco politics. He was a county commissioner and became the first state senator from Pacific County. According to the 1900 census, the population of Ilwaco was over 1,000 people. At this time it had two general stores, two grocery stores, two hotels, two restaurants, three saloons, eight other varied businesses, and a newspaper, the *Pacific Journal*. Ilwaco also had three churches, an opera house, and a Fraternity Hall, where all the fraternal organizations met on different days of the week. Ilwaco was also one of the few towns in the state at the time that was totally free of debt.

The oldest and largest hotel was the Hotel Delavan, which opened in 1872. It was run by Mrs. Curley and was purchased in 1900 by Mrs. Augusta Hayden, who added a second story and refurbished the rest of the building. It was well known for its cleanliness and for its wonderful food. Its name was later changed to the Gilson Hotel.

Other hotels in Ilwaco were the Bay View House, built by Jonathan Stout and purchased by Rees Williams in 1875, and the Central Hotel, built in 1880. In 1914 the Central Hotel was owned by Mrs. Mary McIntosh and was advertised as having the "Best Meals in Town for 25 cents."

Since Ilwaco was mostly a fisherman's town, it experienced much of the violence between the gill-netters and fish trappers. This continued until 1935 when fish traps were banned in the state of Washington. The expansion of the trolling fleet, however, kept Ilwaco's economy from feeling the effects of the loss of the traps. During this time, the population of Ilwaco dropped to just over 600 people, but during the summers and fishing seasons the population almost doubled. After World War II, the sports fishing industry increased and brought people not only to Ilwaco, but to the entire peninsula as well. The size of the mooring basin continued to increase to make room for additional boats coming into the area. It was with this expansion that Ilwaco became known as the "Salmon Fishing Capital of the World." Beginning in the 1980s, the salmon fishing industry slowly declined due to legislation, restrictions, and depletion of salmon in the river. Ilwaco then experienced a depression with many businesses closing their doors.

Today, the town is slowly reinventing itself. With the increase in ocean fishing, as well as the museum and the shops and restaurants established around the mooring basin, Ilwaco is fast becoming a more popular place to visit.

Chinookville/Chinook

Chinookville is thought to have been the first settlement in Pacific County. It was originally a Chinook Indian village located below Point Ellice where Robert Gray dropped anchor in 1792. After visiting with the Chinooks, Gray traded with them for many furs and headed downriver. His ship anchored in the deep water just off Fort Canby and eventually headed out to sea.

On November 15, 1805, Lewis and Clark arrived on the beach of Chinookville in their canoes. Lewis's journals relate that 36 houses were in the village and the population was about 280. The explorers noticed that the Chinook had some tools and implements, indicating they had already traded with Europeans. They camped for ten days, explored the area, and then moved to the south side of the river for the winter.

In 1831 the missionaries Father DeSmet and Father Blanchette visited Chinookville. They converted many of the Chinook to the Catholic faith and in December of 1848, Father Joseph Lionnet received a mission land grant. The mission he established was named Stella Maris, meaning "Star of the Sea." A Methodist missionary also spent some time in this area preaching to the Indians.

In the 1840s, the Columbia River area attracted a few settlers who stayed in Chinookville. Many of the people living in the area were trappers who worked for the Hudson Bay Company. The company built a store and trading post in Chinookville, which ran for about ten years and was operated by Rocque Ducheney, a French-Canadian. The store and trading post attracted many more to the area.

The county seat was moved from Pacific City to Chinookville in 1853, when Washington became its own territory. A later election transferred the county seat to Oysterville in 1855.

In 1844 Captain Scarborough, who had been master of one of the Hudson Bay vessels, took a donation land claim of 643 acres from the government. His claim was located on a portion of the ancestral home of Chief Comcomally. Captain Scarborough was a Scotchman and a river pilot who ran a cattle herd of 150 head and cultivated a large orchard and garden. Several hawthorn trees were planted, with one tree growing to about 50 feet. During the spring, many people from the peninsula visited to view the trees when they flowered. When it bloom, the large hawthorn tree became a landmark for fishermen on the river.

In 1897, the tree was cut down to make room for the batteries of Fort Columbia. Many in the area were very upset at the removal of this landmark and it is said that the people of Chinook planted cuttings from it; several hawthorn trees present in town today are reported to have grown from these cuttings.

Washington Hall surveyed and platted the town of Chinookville in 1850. The land Hall envisioned as a town was the primary settlement of the Chinook Indians, who had lived in the location for centuries.

Hall had been the surveyor for Elijah White at Pacific City, which could well be where his idea to form the town of Chinookville came from. The location of Chinookville provided easy access to fishing grounds and to Astoria across the river. Hall tried to drive out the Indians so he could control all of the land and sell it to new settlers coming into this area. The natives wanted Hall off their land, but were unsuccessful in their attempts to remove him.

The first to purchase land were employees of the Hudson Bay Company. A company store had been built at Chinookville in 1840 to trade with the Chinooks for furs and to provide supplies to trappers and others in the area.

By 1855, Hall had deeded all of his property to his four-year-old son Sylvester, and his two-year-old daughter Elizabeth. He did this to protect his property interest: when people tried to collect for debts he owed, the records showed that he had no property. Hall remained his childrens' legal guardian and continued to sell lots under their names until he left the territory in 1862.

With the increasing numbers of white men living at Chinookville, an increase of there diseases reduced the population of the Chinook to a very few. Eventually even the name Chinookville faded in favor of the name McGowan, after P.J. McGowan, who homesteaded downstream from the old Chinook village. In 1853, McGowan purchased over 300 acres that had been part of the Stella Maris mission grant for the price of $1,200. At this location in 1864, he built one of the first canneries on the Columbia River. This cannery packed brands such as Keystone, Cascade, and Blue Ribbon. Even as Chinookville was dying, a community downriver named Chinook was beginning.

Founding and Settlement

Chinook, also located on Baker's Bay, was famed throughout the United States for its salmon fishing. Gillnet fishing and seining were the two dominant methods of angling until the 1800s, when fish traps were introduced. This was a common way to fish in Scandinavia, and with many Scandinavians living in Chinook, the method became very popular there as well. Trapping fish was very successful, with huge runs being caught in each trap. Scows lined up in front of Chinook to receive the fish from the trappers and transport them to Astoria and other canneries on the river. Individual trappers could sell salmon in any quantity to the people on the scows. Prices were agreed upon at the beginning of the season each year, which ran from May 1 to August 25. At the conclusion of the season, trappers had little to do after the nets were put away. It was then that they and their families would travel to Astoria, Ilwaco, or Chinook to settle financially with the canneries and place orders for the coming winter's supplies. Entertainment, a carnival, and a regatta officially ended the fishing season.

Chinook had no roads to begin with, so all transportation was by boat. At low tide the beach could be traveled on, but the rocks and soft sand made walking difficult. In 1886, the early settlers built a road along the north side of the Chinook River. By 1891, a bridge was completed across the river, forming a land route to Ilwaco. The money to complete it had been raised by the public. At this time, there was no road to McGowan. The transportation route consisted of a trail over the hill or by boat.

Mail for the entire peninsula was received at Chinook until 1900. Later, the mail was brought to Ilwaco by boat and distributed there for all points along the peninsula and Chinook. After 1900, a mail route was operated between Ilwaco and Chinook. Daily trips were made carrying the mail as well as freight and passengers.

School was conducted on the Gile farm in 1879 with Maggy Brown as teacher. Classes were maintained there for a number of years until the building was moved to the Jasper Prest Ranch. Students enjoyed many activities such as mud fights, games, and soccer. In 1897, a new two-story building was constructed, and in 1923 a concrete building was finally erected.

From its beginning, Chinook was a fishing boomtown. By 1892, there were 240 traps in the lower river, most of which were located between Sand Island and the mainland from Chinook Point to Ilwaco. Most were located in front of Chinook and were a major boost to the economy. During some years, as much as $5,000 could be made by each trap during the fishing season.

Chinook was home to the first official salmon hatchery in the state of Washington due to the efforts of Alfred E. Houchen, who had been involved in fisheries on the lower Columbia River since 1868. In 1883, he was asked to move his personal experimental fish hatchery from Bear River to Chinook. This request came from Senator B.A. Seaborg and several salmon fishermen from Ilwaco and Chinook. These people were interested in supporting and maintaining the salmon population on the Columbia. The hatchery was on the Jasper Prest farm on the Chinook. In the first year, approximately 2 million young salmon were released from the hatchery into the river. When Houchen's efforts were successful, the state of Washington took over operations and a permanent hatchery was built.

Chinook developed into a thriving town with a post office, saloon, general store, Methodist Episcopal Church, Lutheran Church, and many large homes. In 1900, the *Chinook Observer* began as a weekly paper. At this time the town was the third largest in Pacific County and the Coleman House was a hotel across from the post office in the business section of town. The Coleman House, owned by James and Sophronia Coleman, was noted for its delicious cuisine and well-furnished rooms. Another house offering room and food to travelers was the Bundy House.

Most everyone in town never had it so good. From 1900–1905, the population grew to nearly 700 and the business section expanded rapidly. Other elements such as the growth of Fort Columbia helped the economy as well. During the Spanish American War hundreds of soldiers were brought to guard the mouth of the Columbia River. Farming, dairy cows, logging, the building of the railway, and the birth of the deep-sea trolling fleet all added to the economic explosion. Chinook at this time was "the richest town per capita" on the Pacific Coast.

By 1930, Chinook had such businesses as the Sunfreze Fountain and Lunch, Chinook Service Station, Dan Williams Merchandise, North Shore Telephone Company, Becken's Confectionery, The Chinook Packing Company, Stilwell's Sanitary Market, and The Ocean Beach Transportation Company, among others.

In 1933, an initiative to ban fish traps and seining was brought to a vote, and by 1935 traps and drag seines were banned in Washington. At this time, the Chinook Fish Hatchery was also closed, which was devastating for the community. With only the payrolls of Fort Columbia, the logging camps, and the farms contributing to the economy, a much lower standard of living prevailed in the area. Chinook today has become a sleepy town that maintains ties to the fishing industry, with an excellent mooring basin.

East of the former site of Chinookville and Megler is a cove called Knappton Cove, also known by the name Hungry Harbor. The Eureka & Epicure Packing Company, a cannery, was located here until the U.S. government bought the site for $8,000 in 1899. The following year, a system was installed that brought water from a spring on the hill down to the site. Plans were to build a quarantine officer's cottage there, along with immigrant barracks, a hospital, and a steamer for use by medical officers in boarding incoming vessels.

From 1899 until 1938 this was the location of a U.S. Public Health Service quarantine station. Because of concerns about the spread of epidemic disease, immigrants were checked for diseases such as cholera, yellow fever, and small pox. Physicians inspected each person entering the country for both disease and mental deficiency. If an immigrant was ill, they were usually hospitalized until well and then admitted to the country. If the immigrant was healthy, they bathed and their belongings and clothes were fumigated. If a ship came into the station and any of the passengers or crew was found to be ill, the entire vessel was quarantined and required to fly a yellow flag that warned others there was disease on board. There was a hospital on shore and stretching out into the water were pilings holding residential quarters for people in quarantine along with the buildings where immigrants were processed. Most of these buildings had formerly been part of the Epicurean Cannery.

More than 300,000 people entered the United States at this station. From here they scattered around the Pacific Northwest, but many stayed on the peninsula and especially in Astoria to fish or work in the canneries. Many of them were Scandinavian, but many others were Chinese, who often worked in the canneries only until they could put together enough money to return home with a tidy savings. Today there is a small museum on the site and it is listed on the National Register of Historic Places.

Chapter Three

MILITARY PRESENCE

ON THE PENINSULA

The Long Beach Peninsula, because of its location at the mouth of the Columbia River, was long an important military locale. It was the site of two former military forts that can be visited today to learn more about the Coastal Defense System at the mouth of the Columbia. Along with Fort Stevens in Oregon, Fort Columbia and Fort Canby on the Long Beach Peninsula were the defense outposts for the U.S. Army in this area. The peninsula is also the location of two lighthouses, which are located at Cape Disappointment and North Head. Cape Disappointment is also the location of a U.S. Coast Guard station and the National Motor Life Boat School. The Coast Guard is the modern embodiment of the U.S. Life Saving Service, which was formerly located at Cape Disappointment and just north of Long Beach at Klipsan Beach. Both the need for navigational aids such as the lighthouses and for life saving services have always been important to the area. Where the Columbia River and the Pacific Ocean meet is one of the most dangerous marine areas on the West Coast, known by many as the Graveyard of the Pacific.

Columbia River

The Columbia River is approximately 1,210 miles long, beginning in Columbia Lake in British Columbia, Canada, and ending at the Pacific Ocean. The main tributaries of the Columbia are the Okanogan, Kootenai, Clark Fork, Snake, and Willamette Rivers. The watershed area is approximately 259,000 square miles, and the ebb discharge at the mouth of the river averages 1,350,000 cubic feet per second.

The Columbia River bar has changed over time. The length of the bar is over six miles, spanning the area between Cape Disappointment and Clatsop Spit, approximately one and a half miles beyond a line between the North and South Jetties. The bar face is where the shallow water of the bar ends and drops into deeper water.

Pacific Coastal Defenses

Coastal defense at the mouth of the Columbia was centered at Fort Stevens in Oregon and at Fort Columbia and Fort Canby in Washington. Army engineers surveyed the coast in 1850, looking for defendable harbors. They found only four deep harbors on the Pacific Coast: San Diego, San Francisco, Puget Sound, and the mouth of the Columbia.

According to the U.S. War Department Document #508, *The Coordination of the Mobile and Coast Artillery Units of the Army in the National Defense*, from 1916:

> Our coast artillery is primarily organized for defensive operations. Some of its functions are:
>
> a. To prevent naval occupation of important strategic and commercial harbors.
>
> b. To prevent naval bombardment of such cities and military and naval bases as are protected by seacoast fortifications.
>
> c. To furnish a strong, fortified base from which submarines and other naval vessels acting on the offensive, may operate.
>
> d. To repel a fleet supporting a landing in force within range of the guns of a fortified harbor.
>
> e. To cooperate with the mobile troops in the landward defense of seacoast fortifications.

The main defenses of the Columbia River were built between 1885 and 1910. Prior to that time, earthen batteries were in place. The building of the first earthen batteries was seen as essential because of the Civil War and also the need to defend U.S. territory from Great Britain. The Coastal Artillery Corps was founded as a branch of the U.S. Army in 1907. But by 1916, many foreign warships could out-range existing harbor defense weapons. Because they were obsolete, the Coastal Artillery forts at this time were mainly being used as Army training and enlistment centers. From 1920 to 1938, the Columbia River forts were put on caretaker status. During the next ten years the forts were reactivated and newer longer-range weapons replaced obsolete artillery. The Coastal Artillery Corp was eliminated in 1950, and most of the large guns were considered surplus or demolished for scrap metal.

Fort Columbia

Fort Columbia, just east of the town of Chinook, was built on a point of land called "Chenoke Point," or Chinook Point. But the Chinook Point and the Columbia River of 200 years ago were much different from those of today. Then, the term Chinook Point is thought to have referred to the land from Point Ellis to an area near the present town of Chinook. Much of that land is gone now, swept away by the powerful currents of the river. Lieutenant W.R. Broughton named this hilly site in 1792 after the Chinook village that was located near it. This village referred to by Broughton was what was later called Chinookville.

Just northeast of the present Chinook Point is a hill approximately 850 feet high that had been called Chinook Hill or Red Patch. The latter name came from the large amount of ferns that grew there and turned red when they died in the winters. This could be seen on the river from a long distance. When Captain James A. Scarborough received a donation land claim of 643 acres in the area, the name of the hill was changed to Scarborough Hill or Scarborough Head. Later the name was shortened to Scarboro Hill, which it is still known by today. Scarborough moved to the site to build a house and farm, which was well established by 1848. He died in 1855, preceded in death by his wife Ann, who died in 1852. There is a legend that just before the captain died he told his Native-American servant the hiding place of his valuables and money. It is said that she was only to tell the location to an "Englishman." The legend holds that Captain Scarborough's treasure is still hidden somewhere on his property. It has been looked for over the years but has not yet been found.

When Scarborough died, James Birnie from the Hudson Bay Company was appointed guardian of Scarborough's two minor sons, Robert and Edwin. Representing the two sons, he sold the farm and property for $1,250 to Rocque Ducheney, who was in charge of the Hudson Bay Company's store in Chinookville. Several years after purchasing the property, Ducheney died. In 1863 the U.S. government, represented by Colonel Rene Edward de Russy, attempted to purchase the land from Rocque Ducheney's wife. It was the next year before the government was finally able to purchase the land for $2,000 plus an additional $1,000 to Mrs. Ducheney for signing a quitclaim deed stating that she held no interest in the property. The final deed was recorded on March 13, 1867.

THE LONG BEACH PENINSULA

Construction on the Coastal Defense fortifications at Fort Columbia did not begin until at least 1896, almost 30 years after the government purchased the land. Before construction could begin, the government needed to build a cement plant, railroad, wharf, and quarters for the workers who would finish the project. In 1897, those workers began to excavate for the first of Fort Columbia's batteries. On April 25 of the following year, two L.F. model 1896 disappearing guns were mounted in the battery and construction of the concrete base for a third gun was completed about the same time.

The battery holding these original three guns was later known as Battery Ord, after Lieutenant Jules G. Ord of the 6th U.S. Infantry. Ord was killed in action at the Battle of San Juan Hill during the Spanish-American War. The guns occupying the battery named in his honor remained in place until after World War I, when they were removed as obsolete.

After completion of the first battery, the fort was turned over to the command at Fort Stevens to guard and maintain. Eleven men were sent from Fort Stevens from Company M, 3rd Artillery, becoming the first troops stationed at Fort Columbia.

By 1900, two additional batteries were built. They were Battery Crenshaw, which held three rapid-fire guns; and Battery Murphy, which held two 6-inch disappearing guns. Battery Crenshaw was named for Captain Frank F. Crenshaw of the 28th Infantry of the U.S. Volunteers, who was killed on August 28, 1900 from wounds received in action in the Philippines during the Spanish-American War. Battery Murphy was named for Captain William L. Murphy of the 39th Infantry of the U.S. Volunteers, who was also killed in the war in the Philippine Islands on August 14, 1900.

In 1899, the U.S. government purchased an additional 86 acres in order to build barracks, officers' quarters, a hospital, and an administration building. By 1902 all the buildings needed to meet the requirements of the soldiers and officers of Fort Columbia were completed. A gymnasium was added in 1906 to provide a recreational area for the men stationed at the fort.

The first permanent troops were sent to the fort in June of 1903. This initial group from the 33rd Company of the Coastal Artillery was made up of one officer and 23 soldiers. Eventually there were four officers and approximately 100 men stationed there. The first commanding officer of Fort Columbia was Captain Brooke Payne.

Military Presence on the Peninsula

In August of 1911, a night target practice was scheduled to allow the troops to practice firing at vessels on the Columbia River. Boats were warned to stay clear of the area of the river downstream of Fort Columbia during this time. A tug pulled a target that was lit up by the fort's searchlights and fired on 18 times. A second series of 18 shots was completed a short time later, at which time the searchlights were turned off indicating that the target practice was over and ships could again enter the restricted area. The test was noted as a success.

At the beginning of World War I, many more troops were sent to Fort Columbia and the other forts at the mouth of the river to reinforce the military security of the area. After the war, the numbers of troops dwindled until only a small group of soldiers designated as caretakers were assigned there. The only major activity was during the two weeks when the National Guard trained at Fort Columbia during the summer.

During World War II, the numbers of troops increased again at all the harbor defenses of the Columbia. Fort Columbia became the controlling station for the mines that ran across the river providing protection against enemy ships coming up the river. A new one, Battery 246, was constructed housing two 6-inch guns on barbette carriages during this time. But battery 246 was never fully completed and at the end of the war, the mines and controls were removed. After World War II Fort Columbia and the other Coastal Defense forts had become obsolete when new strategies for defense in the form of ships and air support became commonplace.

In 1947, Fort Columbia, along with Fort Stevens and Fort Canby, were listed by the War Department as surplus property. Their guns were removed, and in 1948 the Washington State Parks and Recreation Commission applied to the U.S. Government for the fort. On May 12, 1950, most of the property was transferred to Washington State Parks, at which time it became Fort Columbia Historical State Park. A dedication ceremony was held on June 17, 1951, and work began soon after on a museum at the main barracks building. People from all over the peninsula and surrounding areas donated items for the museum, which was completed and opened in June of 1954. The museum is still open, and the park has also opened one of the officer's homes to visitors. This house, called the "Commander's House," has been set up to show what it might have looked like during the earliest period of the fort's occupation.

THE LONG BEACH PENINSULA

Fort Canby

Fort Canby, just west of Ilwaco, was another of the harbor defenses of the Columbia. Originally called Fort Cape Disappointment, it was renamed on January 28, 1875, for General Edward R.S. Canby, who was killed in the Modoc Indian wars.

For many years in the nineteenth century it was known that the West Coast was not defended very effectively against the possibility of attack. As early as 1852 an order was approved by President Millard Fillmore to establish a fort at Cape Disappointment, but no action was taken at that time. In a report to Lieutenant General Winfield Scott in 1860, General George Wright highlighted the fact that the settlements along the Columbia River were open to attack because of a lack of defenses at the mouth of the river. He suggested that the site at Cape Disappointment should be purchased as one of the points of defense. Engineers were eventually sent to survey the entrance of the river to look for ideal sites for building batteries for coastal protection. A site on the Oregon side was considered the best location for the defense of the river, with Cape Disappointment as a second choice. In 1862, initial construction commenced at Point Adams in Oregon and also at Cape Disappointment. However, the Cape Disappointment site presented a challenge in that the main point of defense was located at the lighthouse, over 200 feet above the level of the water.

George H. Elliot, an engineer with the Department of the Pacific, was in charge of building the battery to house the guns. He had a difficult time finding workers, as many local men were off searching for gold during the gold rush of that period. By offering what was considered very good pay for the time, he eventually found enough laborers and by 1864 several 8- and 10-inch guns were delivered to the cape for installation.

The "Lighthouse Battery" eventually housed seven guns: two 8-inch and four 10-inch guns, which were lined up behind parapets along the grounds around and near the lighthouse. The battery had another, larger gun—a 15-inch Rodman smoothbore—that could shoot a 315-pound projectile as far as two miles or a projectile as large as 450 pounds for a shorter distance. This 50,000-pound weapon was mounted on a center pintle in front of the lighthouse. A letter printed in the Salem *Oregon Statesman* on November 14,

1864, stated that the gun was hauled up the hill and that there would eventually be 22 guns mounted at this location. These guns were actually designated for three batteries: the "Lighthouse" or Tower battery, Left Battery, and Center Battery. These three stood guard over the entrance to the Columbia until they were dismantled in 1900. New defenses were built at Fort Canby four years later and battery Harvey Allen was built just north of Cape Disappointment lighthouse, designed to overlook and guard the Pacific and the entrance to the Columbia. Battery Elijah O'Flyng was built to the east of the lighthouse and was aimed at the river.

Both batteries housed guns with disappearing carriages. Battery Allen had three guns and O'Flyng had two. Battery Allen was named for Lieutenant Colonel Harvey A. Allen of the 2nd U.S. Artillery, who fought in the Mexican and Civil Wars and died on September 20, 1882. Battery O'Flyng was named for Ensign Elijah T. O'Flyng of the 23rd Infantry, who died September 18, 1814, of wounds he received in the war of 1812.

The fort was gradually built up so that by 1921 the small bay in front of it was lined with officer's houses, barracks, a hospital, cemetery, stable, wagon house, guard house, ordinance storage, a bakery, and other supporting buildings. This same location was shared with the Cape Disappointment lighthouse keeper's residence and the Lifesaving/Coast Guard station. The majority of this area today is taken up by the Coast Guard station and its family housing.

In 1917, construction was started on Battery Guenther. Guenther would be a mortar battery built just to the east and down the hill from Battery Allen. Battery Guenther housed four 12-inch mortars and a 6-inch gun that was moved from Battery Allen. In April of 1922, upon the completion of Battery Guenther, Captain Carlson, commander of the Coastal Defense at the mouth of the Columbia, along with a squad of men from Fort Stevens, came to Fort Canby to test fire the new mortars. Each of the four 12-inch guns was fired two times with shot weighing 1,046 pounds each. It was noted that the firing of the massive pieces broke several windows at the new battery and in the houses at Fort Canby. Battery Guenther was the last seacoast defense mortar battery built in the United States.

After World War I, a caretaking crew consisting of one sergeant and two enlisted personnel manned Fort Canby. It remained on caretaker status until

1939. On February 21, 1941, Fort Canby was re-activated for World War II, but the only action seen at the mouth of the Columbia was on June 21, 1942, when a Japanese submarine fired nine shells at Fort Stevens across the river. This was the only time since the War of 1812 that an American coastal fortification had been fired on by a foreign enemy vessel.

In 1943 a new battery called Battery 247 was built on McKenzie Head just north of Harvey Allen. Mounted in the new battery were two 6-inch long-range rapid-fire rifles. The usefulness of this new battery was short lived. It was activated in March of 1945, but by July of the same year the Army began to deactivate it. Within two years Fort Canby was declared excess and by October of 1947 all Army personnel were transferred out. Fort Canby became the property of the Army Corps of Engineers and in 1948, 491 acres were transferred to the U.S. Coast Guard. This became Coast Guard Station Cape Disappointment. In 1966, 725 acres were leased to the Washington State Parks Commission, and the next year they were able to lease an additional 542 acres. With the accumulation of additional land, 1,882 acres are now owned by the state of Washington in what now comprises Fort Canby State Park.

Wartime

During World War I and World War II, Coastal Artillery units were assigned to patrol the beaches of the Long Beach Peninsula as well as other Pacific coastal areas. These men patrolled and kept watch by foot, horseback, vehicles, and observation balloons. Because of their location on the Pacific coast and because of fears of attack during wartime, people living on the peninsula were also very important in assisting the military with national defense.

On February 13, 1941, a blackout drill was scheduled from Megler to Stackpole Harbor. This blackout was a national defense drill designed to make the area invisible at night to any enemy bombers. People were asked to turn out all lights when the siren blew or bell rang at exactly 7:45 pm. If lights were needed, then residents were to blanket all windows. An Army–Air Force airplane soared over the area to check the effectiveness of the drill. Many locals were enlisted to coordinate the drill in their communities.

According to the February 21, 1941 *Ilwaco Tribune*, the drill was a complete success. Two large bombers flew over the peninsula and were lit up by the searchlights at Ilwaco, Long Beach, and Klipsan as they headed back and forth over the peninsula. Manning the searchlights were men from Battery G of the 249th Coast Artillery. The American Legion, VFW, fire departments, Boy Scouts, 4-H, and the Peninsula Council for National Defense also helped during the drill.

The effects of a real blackout were seen in December of 1941 when Pearl Harbor was attacked. Worried that the continental United States or its vessels would also be attacked, all ships were ordered back to U.S. ports and the coastline was ordered to black out. The order for radio silence along with the blackout also shut down all the aids to navigation, including the lighthouses. On December 10, the ship *Mauna Ala*, which had been en route to Hawaii, wrecked on the Oregon side of the Columbia River. When the ship headed back to port after abandoning its voyage to Hawaii, the crew was unaware that there was a blackout in effect that would affect the navigational aids. A passing vessel had signaled the *Mauna Ala* to stop, but the message was hard to read and not understood due to the fog.

After initially slowing, the freighter picked up speed thinking it was in close proximity to the Columbia River lightship. Shortly afterward the crew sighted breakers and according to the *Ilwaco Tribune*, the ship "drove ashore head-on . . . jarring hard and coming to rest 700 yards from the water's edge." The breaking waves eventually pushed the ship over on its side and within two days the *Mauna Ala* broke apart under the heavy surf. The Captain and crew were all rescued by the Coast Guard and taken to Point Adams. The *Mauna Ala* was carrying 60,000 Christmas trees to the people in Hawaii as well as food, cargo, and lumber. This incident led to an increased appreciation for the value of the navigational aids and lighthouses at the mouth of the Columbia.

Lighthouses

Four lighthouses have been located near the mouth of the Columbia River: Cape Disappointment, 1856; Point Adams, 1875; North Head, 1898; and Desdemona Sands, 1902. Point Adams was discontinued in 1899 and Desdemona Sands in 1934, and today nothing remains of either lighthouse. The two remaining lighthouses, Cape Disappointment and North Head, continue to provide visual markers for ships that approach this area.

THE LONG BEACH PENINSULA

Cape Disappointment lighthouse was built on solid rock at the very point where the Columbia River meets the Pacific Ocean. A government survey was done in 1848 and Cape Disappointment was selected as one of the eight sites for a lighthouse on the West Coast. Before there was a lighthouse, people notched trees and used white rags tied to trees during the day and bonfires at night to help guide ships across the bar into the river.

A setback in the construction of the lighthouse occurred in the fall of 1853, when the bark *Oriole* wrecked coming over the bar. The ship was carrying the building supplies for the new lighthouse when it went aground on a sand bar as it tried to enter the river. The waves pushed the ship back and forth on the sand until a hole opened in the hull. The current and outgoing tide carried it out toward the ocean, where it filled full of water and sank. It took several months for new supplies to be shipped so that construction of the new lighthouse could continue. In 1854 the tower, which had already been built, was found to be too small for the light and it had to be rebuilt. Cape Disappointment lighthouse was finally completed on October 15, 1856, at a cost of $38,500. The tower stands 53 feet high and is located 220 feet above the water.

The first light installed in the tower was a Fresnel lens of the first order. It was lit by five oil wicks, which used five gallons each night to keep the light going. It was the duty of the lighthouse keeper to keep oil in the lamp, trim the wicks, and maintain the light and lens. Lighthouses used a variety of types of oil over the years to keep the luminescence going, including whale oil, colza oil (rapeseed), lard oil, and kerosene. In 1898, the Fresnel lens was replaced by a smaller fourth-order Barbier and Benard, and the old lens was moved to North Head lighthouse.

The Fresnel lens is now on display in the maritime exhibit at the Lewis and Clark Interpretive Center. At one time, the lighthouse also had a 1,600-pound bronze bell that was used as a fog signal. It was not very effective and was eventually taken out because there were so many dead spots where the signal could not be heard due to the cliff formations of the cape.

In 1921, the Lighthouse Service was considering discontinuing the lighthouse at Cape Disappointment. The reason given was economy. It was thought that with new technology and the presence of river pilots, the lighthouse was no longer needed to safely maneuver the Columbia River bar. This controversy was protested by everyone in the area due to the necessity of the light for the safety of fishermen who regularly crossed the bar. Everyone was encouraged to contact their congressmen and write letters to protest this action. Finally in a letter dated March 24, 1922, the people of the peninsula learned that C.H. Huston, acting secretary of commerce, had decided that "no further action as to the discontinuance of this light" would be taken at the time. The lighthouse continues to be of service to the present day.

Of the eight original lighthouses constructed on the West Coast, Cape Disappointment lighthouse is one of only three that have survived. The U.S. Coast Guard presently maintains Cape Disappointment lighthouse and the light at North Head.

North Head was built in 1898 and lit on May 16 of that year. It is located just two miles north of Cape Disappointment and has a 65-foot tower and stands 194 feet above the water line. On August 1, 1902, a weather station was established at North Head by the Department of Agriculture. This was an official U.S. weather station and was staffed 24 hours a day. Weather and surf conditions were observed and taken every four hours and the information relayed to the Weather Service in Portland.

On January 5, 1906, the U.S. Weather Bureau at North Head was destroyed by a lightning strike at about 2:00 p.m. One bolt of lightning hit the tower, came through the roof, and burned out the wiring. Another bolt came through the window and destroyed the instruments. The Weather Bureau staff person on duty, a Mr. Kelliher, was also injured. The Weather Bureau station was not able to operate again for about two weeks.

According to the official records, North Head is claimed to be one of the windiest places on the West Coast. In 1921, several gusts estimated at 160 miles per hour destroyed all of the weather equipment, blew off roofs, and downed many trees. This area is also one of the foggiest places on the West Coast with an average 160 foggy days each year. The weather station was removed in 1955.

A wireless signal station was built at North Head in 1912 and provided weather information to the batteries of Fort Canby and to ships that passed by. It was able to send and receive messages up to 3,000 miles. An upgrade to the signal station was completed in 1912. With these improvements, it became the most powerful wireless station on the Pacific coast. The upgraded station was described in a December 23, 1911 *Ilwaco Tribune* article as "two steel masts, situated 500 feet apart [that] tower to a height of 300 feet. Heretofore a single tower of wooden construction of 180 feet in height has been made to answer the purpose since the wireless station was established." The improvements effectively doubled the station's range, allowing it to receive and send messages as far away as 6,000 miles.

The first light for North Head was the Fresnel lens that had previously been in the Cape Disappointment lighthouse. It was 80,000 candlepower and could be seen by ships for at least 20 miles. In 1932, a duck, perhaps blinded by the light, flew into the lens and broke a window in the lighthouse as well as chipping some of the prisms on the lens. When the Coast Guard took over responsibility for the lights from the U.S. Lighthouse Service, it made extensive changes to North Head, installing first a fourth-order lens in 1939 and later a Crous-Hinds marine beacon. This light produces 1.2 million candlepower and is visible to ships heading south down the coast for a very long distance. The only time North Head light was ever turned off was after the Japanese submarine attack on Fort Stevens in 1942. At 12:35 a.m. on June 22, it was turned off temporarily to prevent another attack. After the bombing of Pearl Harbor, the Army also built observation and searchlight stations at North Head.

There was a great controversy in 1912 when the government wanted to cut down trees to help pay for a road to North Head Lighthouse and to Fort Canby. An article in the June 2, 1935 *Oregon Sunday Journal* stated:

> Another feature of interest is the highway from Ilwaco to within a half mile of North head lighthouse. The last half-mile is plank road leading over government property. At the lighthouse visitors may look through the government's telescope, whose powerful lens picks out objects as far south as Tillamook Head. From the North Head road junction it is one and one half miles to Fort Canby, where the Cape Disappointment life saving station, lookout and lighthouse are located. The plank road into Fort Canby is to be replaced soon with a regular road with the aid of the CCC (Civilian Conservation Corps) camp.

Lighthouse Keepers

Lighthouse keepers were employed and assigned under the U.S. Lighthouse Service. In order to be a lightkeeper one was required to be between the ages of 18 and 50, be able to read, write, and keep books, do manual labor, sail a boat, and have mechanical ability in order to keep the equipment in good repair. Preference in hiring went to retired sea captains or mates who had families. Keepers were not allowed to do anything that would take away from their duties. They were responsible for polishing brass, cleaning glass, painting, housekeeping, yard work, and maintenance and repair of machinery. In addition, the clockwork mechanism that fed fuel to the light had to be cranked by hand every few hours.

Many of the early lenses turned on roller bearings or floated in a bath of mercury. The first order Fresnel lens that was installed at both Cape Disappointment and North Head lighthouses did not turn at all. It was a fixed lens. When the keepers worked in the lantern room, they wore long white aprons to prevent their buttons from scratching the lens. The lens was cleaned every day with a feather duster and a clean linen cloth. The keepers washed it every two months with water, spirits of wine, and a soft rag and would polish it once a year with rouge powder. It was the lighthouse keeper's most important duty to maintain the light and lens so that it would remain visible to both ships at sea and those crossing the bar.

During the early days the keepers received pay and housing. It was also interesting that at North Head the higher the position, the more bulbs a keeper had in the dining room chandelier. The head lighthouse keeper received $800 per year, a single two-story residence, and had a six-bulb chandelier in the dining room. The first assistant received $600 per year and one side of a duplex residence, plus a five-bulb chandelier. The second assistant received $550 per year, the other side of the duplex residence, and a four-bulb chandelier. The keepers' houses, which were very near the lighthouses, can still be seen at North Head, but the keeper's house at Cape Disappointment is no longer there.

There were lighthouse keepers in residence until President Franklin Roosevelt transferred the responsibility of the stations and the keepers to the Coast Guard in 1938.

Lightships

The Columbia River had a lightship stationed at its mouth from the year 1892 to 1979. The first lightship on the Pacific Coast was the Columbia River #50, which was anchored off the mouth of the river in 1892. She was an important aid to navigation to any ship entering or leaving the Columbia for many years until 1899, when she broke anchor during a gale. Several ships attempted to tow the lightship back into the river but none were successful. Columbia River #50 ran aground on the beach just north of Cape Disappointment and several attempts were made to salvage the ship. This was finally accomplished by transporting it on sleds pulled by horses into Baker's Bay. The ship was repaired and put back in service on September 6, 1901.

Columbia River #50 was a 112-foot long sailing ship. The vessel had two boilers that made steam for the fog whistles and operated the mechanism that raised the lights up to the top of the masts. The lights were a group of six lamps circling around the masts. This allowed ships to see the lights from all directions. During the day, the they were put out and lowered into small rooms at the bottom of each mast. A cover was closed over the lights during the day. At night and on low visibility days, the covers came off and they were hoisted up the masts.

Lightship #50 was eventually replaced in 1909 by a more modern vessel, Lightship #88. Lightship #88 was in turn eventually replaced by Lightship #93.

The last lightship to be anchored at the mouth of the Columbia River was the Lightship *Columbia*, #604. It was discontinued from service on November 2, 1979, when it was replaced by a 42-foot navigational buoy officially called "Columbia River Approach Lighted Horn Buoy." The Lightship *Columbia* can be seen at the Columbia River Maritime Museum in Astoria, Oregon, where it is on display.

Jetties

In order to control the channel of the Columbia River and make it safer for ships, a series of jetties was built at the mouth of the river. The first constructed was the south jetty, which can be seen on the Oregon side of the river. Construction began in 1885, with the first stage being completed ten years later in 1895. This project resulted in a jetty 4.5 miles long.

The North Jetty on the Washington side of the river was contracted in 1913, started in 1914, and completed in 1917. In order to construct it, buildings, water and sewage facilities, housing, and a railway had to first be built. The channel near Sand Island had to be dredged and a dock built there in order to bring in the supplies and rock needed to build the jetty. A railway had to be built across land from the dock to the site of the jetty. Pilings were driven along the path of the jetty to form a trestle, and the railroad tracks were laid on top of the pilings. Barges loaded with rock were brought downriver to the dock. Small engines pulled the rock-hauling rail cars along the top of the jetty extending into the river, where the cars were able to dump on both sides. This work continued until a massive rock jetty covered the entire trestle.

The jetty was a dangerous place to work because of the heavy equipment, the loose boulders, and all the water surrounding it. In 1914, one of the trackwalkers was swept from the tracks by a large breaker and drowned. Because of the extreme high tide and rough seas that day, after the man was swept off the track, part of the jetty collapsed and a rock car was washed into the water as well. Two others working nearby on the track had to grab the rails to prevent them from also being swept away.

The final length of the North Jetty was approximately 2.3 miles. It was built approximately 30 feet high and 25 feet wide, made up of nearly 3 million tons of rock. The area called Peacock Spit had been under 15 feet of water prior to the jetty being built, but after the construction of the North Jetty, the spit was moved toward the north and eventually filled in the area to an average height of 15 feet above sea level. This accretion of sand added over 1,000 acres to the land between the jetty and North Head. Even more acreage was added to the peninsula as a whole from the jetty's construction.

The Columbia River channel was greatly improved and stabilized by the construction of the jetties. The final construction of North Jetty left an opening approximately 2,000 feet wide, which became the entrance to the river. The depth of this channel was around 40 feet, but in order to maintain this depth the channel required frequent dredging. Because of the increase in the number of large seagoing ships entering the river, the main channel was eventually dredged to 48 feet.

A third jetty, Jetty A, was also constructed to help control the channel. Jetty A, which juts out toward the south into the river near Cape Disappointment, was built between 1932 and 1938.

As one looks out toward the jetties today it can be seen that they are slowly breaking down due to constant exposure to the tremendous currents and waves of the Columbia River and the Pacific Ocean. As this happens, the water washes out the sand held behind the jetties and the channel becomes shallower, requiring dredging on a regular basis. This continued dredging, as well as repair of the three jetties, will help keep the channels open for some time.

United States Life Saving Service

The U.S. Lifesaving Service, under the jurisdiction of the U.S. Treasury Department, built two lifesaving stations on the Long Beach Peninsula. The two outposts were Cape Disappointment built in 1878, and Ilwaco Beach (Klipsan Beach) in 1889.

In 1894, keepers made $900 per year and surf men made from $480 to $600 per year. The Ilwaco Beach Station had one keeper in charge and seven surf men. Surf men had to be less than 48 years old as well as physically fit and able to read and write.

The keepers had administrative responsibilities and had legal authority over shipwrecks and smuggling. According to Article 69 of the Revised Regulations of the Life Saving Service of 1877, keepers had "powers of Inspector of Customs and have authority and are required to take charge of and protect all property saved from any shipwreck at which they may be present." Keepers were also charged with the authority to prevent smuggling and were given a portion of proceeds from the sale of smuggled goods. According to Treasury Department circular No. 66, dated July 2, 1878, "For the detection and seizure of such smuggled goods they will be entitled to such compensation as this department shall award, not exceeding in amount, one half of the net proceeds after deduction of duties, expenses, etc."

The keeper and surf men had very specific duties and rules. A surf man would stand watch in the tower during the day and at night, or on low visibility days two surf men would patrol different directions on the beach, each patrolling three miles from the station and back. Another Treasury

Department circular, No. 155, dated October 12, 1891, was on "Instructions to Employees of the Life-Saving Service Relative to The Use of Signals in Case of Shipwreck." This document instructed employees on how to signal to ships at both night and day. If a surf man discovered a wreck at night, he was required to signal with a red light or rocket to signify "You are seen; assistance will be given as soon as possible." If they swung a white light slowly back and forth or set off a white rocket or Roman candle, it meant "Slack Away." Two lights, a white and a red, swung slowly at the same time or a blue light meant, "Do not attempt to land in your own boats; it is impossible." Two torches burned together at night signified "This is the best place to land." During the day the men would use flags to signal instead of lights.

The crews were called to lifesaving duties by a loud gong. They had a code for the number of gongs or bells they heard: one bell was to call number one of the crew, two bells meant to muster at the usual place, three bells meant man the boat or beach cart, and four bells meant muster for inspection. Rapid striking of the gong signified a fire or other emergency.

The Life Saving Service used a rowing lifeboat in the early days. The boat was pushed out into the breakers and rowed by six surf men to the ship in distress. The lifeboat was transported to the scene of a shipwreck or wherever else it was needed on a wagon pulled by either horses or by manpower. After the railroad was established, the trains were sometimes used to transport the boat, men, and equipment from the Ilwaco Beach Station to the site of an emergency along the beach.

One method of establishing a connection with a shipwreck besides the lifeboat was by using a Lyle gun and breeches buoy. The Lyle gun was a small cannon that would shoot a small line from the shore to the ship in distress. The surf men could then attach a larger line to the small line, which could be pulled aboard the ship. On this larger line a breeches buoy could be attached. This was basically a life ring with what looked like a short pair of pants attached. This buoy could be pulled back and forth, carrying people from the ship to safety on shore.

The lifesaving crews continually held practice drills in front of Fort Canby in the bay and in the surf along the beach. People would often travel to Fort Canby or to Ilwaco Beach to watch their drills.

Cape Disappointment Life Saving Station

The first official lifesaving station on the peninsula was built at Fort Canby near the mouth of the Columbia River. This station was established on September 8, 1877. Prior to an official station being built and manned however, lighthouse keeper Joel Munson started a volunteer station. The official station continued to be manned by volunteers for another five years until 1882, when the first full-time crew was sworn in.

This crew evidently enjoyed the pleasures of a cook at least part of the time and was greatly dismayed when she left to get married. Their sadness was noted in the following poem by Charley L. Gant from the July 25, 1914 *Ilwaco Tribune*:

> "The Lost Cook"
> They have lost their cook at Canby
> And they're sad each spruced up dandy
> Out on Old Cape Disappointment
> They're as sad as sad can be
> They were happy while she tarried
> But she left them to get married
> And there's lots of sobs commingling
> With the salt-besprinkled sea.
>
> They say God never made a
> More superb and gentle lady
> For she seemed just like a mother
> To the Disappointment crew
> But life seems all phony
> Since she took up matrimony
> And quit her job of cooking
> Only just to cook for two.
>
> There's a sorry lot of sinners
> Sitting down to stranger's dinners

And they look forlorn at suppers
Leastwise Weston says they do
And no longer are they genial
Since their cook has gone hymenial
It's hades hot and heavy
With the Disappointment crew.

Eventually this station became the United States Coast Guard Cape Disappointment station. It continues to operate as a Coast Guard station today.

Ilwaco Beach (Klipsan Beach) Life Saving Station

The Ilwaco Beach (Klipsan Beach) Life Saving Station was located 13 miles north of Cape Disappointment on the ocean beach. Its location was important because of the number of wrecks that came ashore in the area and equally critical because of the unbroken visibility possible for several miles each way up and down the beach.

The Ilwaco Beach station was the second station built on the peninsula. The outpost was constructed in 1891 on land purchased from Edwin G. Loomis, the brother of Lewis Loomis, owner of the Ilwaco Railroad & Navigation Company. The first keeper of the Ilwaco Beach station was Richard Turk, who along with seven surf men provided life saving services to the northern end of the peninsula.

In 1912 Captain Theodore Conick, who had been assigned as keeper since 1902, proposed the change in name from Ilwaco Beach to Klipsan Beach. With the advances in technology after World War II, the Coast Guard personnel were transferred out of the station and it thus fell into caretaker status. The government stripped and salvaged the equipment and fixtures, and in 1949 it officially abandoned the Ilwaco Beach/Klipsan Beach Station. Some of the original buildings are still standing at the site, and have since been converted to private homes.

United States Coast Guard

In 1915, the U.S. Department of the Treasury combined the Life Saving Service with the Revenue Cutter Service to form the U.S. Coast Guard.

Coast Guard personnel regularly risk their lives to save boaters, fishermen, and others who require assistance in the waters near the Columbia River. In 1930, after the shipwreck of the *Admiral Benson*, it was noted in an editorial in the *Chinook Observer* that:

> Every Coast Guard station should be provided with an emergency fund for feeding refugees from the sea and with a commissary containing blankets and clothes to be used as the occasions arises. This was made obvious during the last few days in connection with the rescue of the passengers and crew of the ship Admiral Benson.

The writer continued:

> More than a hundred men and women were taken from the ship either by life boat or breeches buoy and landed on the beach at the north jetty. Many of them were wet and cold, but the coast guard could not supply them with dry blankets and clothes because the coast guard does not have them. These rescued men and women then either walked or were transported over the difficult four miles to the Cape Disappointment life saving station. There they were provided with all the coats, and caps and clothing that could be dug out of the closets, but the clothing came so to speak off the backs of the guardsmen themselves—men who are drawing $90 a month.

The victims of the shipwreck were then fed at the Cape dining room. The food had to be purchased by the guardsmen or the volunteers who came from the beach to help. It was noted that while the Coast Guard was usually reimbursed by the company owning the ship, until that payment was made, it came out of the pockets of the men. The editorial stressed that the government should provide supplies for the men to have on hand to take care of shipwreck victims.

Military Presence on the Peninsula

During Prohibition many boats traveled up and down the coastline transporting liquor from Canada to points along the American coast. On January 17, 1922, two men in a 40-foot trawler called the *B&W* ran aground on the north jetty. The Coast Guard crew responded to the ship and found 65 cases of Canadian whisky and four 15-gallon casks. One man was arrested and the other escaped from authorities by following the old cable trail from the landing to North Head and making his way to Ilwaco. Not wanting to wait for the train, he hired a jitney to take him to the ferry landing and from there rode the ferry to Astoria. The police were never able to locate him. According to the *Ilwaco Tribune*, this was "one of the largest liquor hauls ever made at the mouth of the river."

The U.S. Coast Guard Cape Disappointment station is the largest in the Pacific Northwest, providing maritime law enforcement, national security, and rescue and assistance to boats, ships, and persons in an area around the Columbia River mouth and the Long Beach Peninsula.

Also located at Cape Disappointment is the National Motor Lifeboat School. Originally established in 1968 and expanded in 1980, hundreds of Coast Guard personnel have graduated from this school. The Columbia River bar provides students with rough water experience not available at any other location in the United States.

On January 12, 1961, a tragedy known as the Triumph—F/V Mermaid incident took the lives of five members of the Coast Guard and two crew members of the fishing vessel *Mermaid*. According to the official Coast Guard Board of Investigation report the following facts are known:

At approximately 4:15 p.m. on January 12, 1961, Coast Guard Lifeboat Station Cape Disappointment received a distress call from the fishing vessel *Jana Jo* stating that the 34-foot fishing vessel *Mermaid* had lost her rudder and was adrift in the 8- to 15-foot swells on the Columbia River bar. The wind was south-southwest at 35 to 40 knots. The weather was getting worse and gale warnings were posted at 5:00 p.m.

The Coast Guard sent out CG-40564, a 40-foot Coast Guard motor lifeboat, to be followed by CG-36454, a 36-foot motor lifeboat. They were to attempt to get a line on the *Mermaid* before she drifted onto Peacock Spit. It was difficult for the Coast Guardsmen to see the *Mermaid* as it was getting dark and there was a storm. But finally, they were able to locate the fishing vessel and the 40-foot lifeboat took the *Mermaid* in tow.

Because the weather conditions were getting worse, the officer in charge at Cape Disappointment contacted Point Adams to request assistance from its 52-foot lifeboat. The Coast Guard boat with the *Mermaid* in tow was ordered to wait near Buoy #1 for the larger vessel. It arrived at Buoy #1 at approximately 6:15 p.m. and was joined by a 36-foot lifeboat. They waited together until the 52-foot lifeboat from Point Adams joined them at 7:15 p.m., and proceeded to take over the tow.

The smaller lifeboats were experiencing radio difficulties due to the amount of water from the storm and high waves, so communication was difficult. All three Coast Guard vessels and the vessel in tow headed toward the entrance to the river. Near Buoy #7, the 40-foot Coast Guard lifeboat was capsized by a series of large swells. The three crewmembers on board were eventually able to get hold of their overturned lifeboat. As the 36-foot lifeboat came up behind, it found it was taking on water and decided to turn around and head for the lightship instead of trying to cross the rough bar. But as it turned around, it saw the 40-foot lifeboat upside down with the crew clinging to it. The crew of the 36-foot lifeboat was able to grab one of the crew and turned to try to rescue the other two when a wave caused it to collide with the 40-foot boat overturned in the water. The two Coast Guardsmen were quickly taken aboard and the 36-foot lifeboat headed for the lightship. It had been damaged even more from the collision but continued on to the lightship, passing the 52-foot lifeboat with the *Mermaid* in tow. After about an hour, the 36-foot boat with both crews on board made it safely to the lightship.

The 52-foot lifeboat with the *Mermaid* in tow reached Buoy #1 and headed into the river. The towline broke, but they were able to establish another line. This second one broke as well, and the last report had the *Mermaid* drifting toward Peacock Spit. At approximately 8:13 p.m. the *Mermaid* radioed that the 52-foot lifeboat had capsized and that one of the crew had made it to the fishing boat. They also said they were drifting toward Peacock Spit and needed assistance. Another of the crewmembers was swept off the lifeboat and ended up on the beach. A ship in the area reported that it witnessed the *Mermaid* being hit by a wave and disappearing completely. Air, sea, and ground patrols were initiated to look for survivors and victims.

During this one night, seven lives were lost. Two of the victims were Bert Bergman and Stanley Bergman of the fishing vessel *Mermaid*. The five Coast Guardsmen who lost their lives were John Culp, John Hoban, Joseph Petrin, Gordon Sussex, and Ralph Mace.

This is just one example of the members of the U.S. Coast Guard at Cape Disappointment putting their lives on the line to help those needing assistance in the dangerous waters surrounding the Long Beach Peninsula. The peninsula has a long and interesting maritime and military history, conveyed today by several museums in Ilwaco and Chinook. The military presence and maritime activity not only brought economic benefits to the area but also eventually became part of the communities they assisted. Many of those stationed here later settled in the area.

A map of the Long Beach Peninsula.

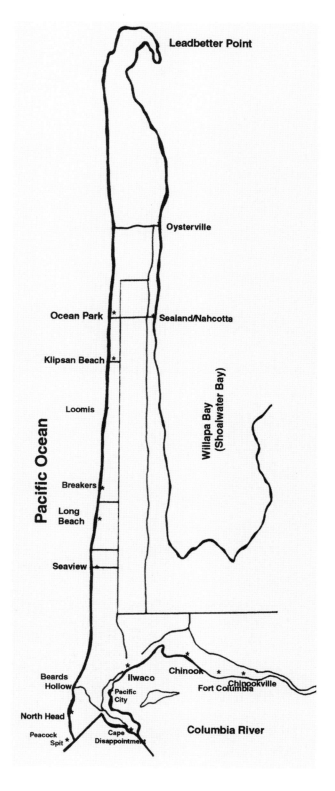

Leadbetter Point

Oysterville

Ocean Park *

Sealand/Nahcotta

Klipsan Beach *

Loomis

Pacific Ocean

Willapa Bay
(Shoalwater Bay)

Breakers *

Long
Beach *

Seaview

Beards
Hollow

Ilwaco

Chinook *

Pacific
City

Fort Columbia *   *
Chinookville

North Head *

Columbia River

Peacock
Spit *

Cape
Disappointment

"The Middle Columbia"
Chinook Indian in a canoe
on the Columbia River
near Chinookville in 1910.
Edward S. Curtis Collection,
No. 3040–10.

A 1910 map of Long Beach Peninsula.

Peninsula College in Oysterville in 1895. The main portion of this building was the former Pacific County Courthouse. The addition was added later.

Nahcotta in 1909. MSCUA, University of Washington Libraries, No. UW23000.

U.S. Life Saving Station, Ilwaco Beach (Klipsan) in 1895. MSCUA, University of Washington Libraries, No. UW14075.

Loading oyster cultch at the port in Nahcotta. The Tribune, *Ilwaco.*

The main street of Long Beach looking south in 1929. Included in the photo are the Long Beach Hotel and Tinker Land Company office.

The Portland Hotel in Long Beach in 1910. It was located just north of the train depot. MSCUA, University of Washington Libraries, No. UW22999.

Crystal Baths in Long Beach in 1910 (that burned down in 1912); the Lyniff Bath House is just behind it. These were both popular places to visit.

The Long Beach Boulevard looking south in 1910. Notice how close the water and driftwood are to the dirt street, which during storms would cover the street.

Part of the 1930's Urban Collection, here is one of the many motels (Urban's Court and later Hill's Motel) on the Long Beach Peninsula. The low area to the left is where the boulevard is now.

The Long Beach schoolhouse in 1915.

In 1910 the Hackney Cottage in Seaview was one of the popular places for tourists to stay.

Train depot and businesses in Seaview in 1910. MSCUA, University of Washington Libraries, No. UW23001.

Ilwaco School in 1914.

Early photo of Ilwaco looking south toward the Columbia River in 1897. MSCUA, University of Washington Libraries, No. UW12704.

St. Mary's Catholic Church near McGowan. This church was built just west of the old Stella Maris Mission grant. The Tribune, *Ilwaco.*

Cape Disappointment Lighthouse Battery looking west toward where the Columbia River and Pacific Ocean meet. Washington State Parks and Recreation Commission.

Military medical staff at Fort Columbia in dress uniform. Note the small kitten being held by one of the staff. Washington State Parks and Recreation Commission.

U.S. Army Reserves during training at Fort Columbia. Washington State Parks and Recreation Commission.

West Battery guns looking out over the Columbia River. A perfect place to enjoy the view. The Washington State Parks and Recreation Commission.

Fort Canby military buildings in 1890. Washington State Parks and Recreation Commission.

Ladies dressed up for an outing at the Cape Disappointment Lighthouse Battery. They are leaning against "Ole Betsy," the 15-inch smoothbore Rodman cannon.

The view from Fort Canby/Cape Disappointment Lighthouse Battery in 1913. This panorama looks north toward McKenzie Head.

The Plank road to North Head Lighthouse in 1903.

A postcard of a life-saving crew returning from surf drills near Long Beach in 1920.

The View from North Head lighthouse toward the North Jetty. Below is Benson Beach. Urban Collection.

An excursion tour in a horse-drawn surf wagon heading down the beach in 1892. MSCUA, University of Washington Libraries, No. La Roche 177.

Terminus of the railroad in Nahcotta and one of the Ilwaco Railroad and Navigation Company engines and car. The Tribune, *Ilwaco.*

Terminus of the railroad at Megler on the Columbia River in 1900. This is where the T.J. Potter and ferries would stop to drop off passengers so they could catch the train to the Peninsula.

One of Captain Elfving's ferries, the Tourist #2, transporting cars and passengers between Astoria and Megler.

Oystermen working in Willapa Bay. The Tribune, *Ilwaco.*

Cultch in place to catch oyster spat in Willapa Bay. The Tribune, *Ilwaco.*

An Oyster-harvesting operation in Willapa Bay in 1940. MSCUA, University of Washington Libraries, UW22998.

Cars disembarking from a ferry at Megler landing in the 1960s. The Tribune, *Ilwaco.*

Fishermen taking salmon out of a fish trap in Baker's Bay. MSCUA, University of Washington Libraries, No. UW12665.

Wet harvesting of cranberries, which are pushed on to a conveyor belt and emptied into a truck. Urban Collection.

Salmon gillnet boats at anchor at Point Ellis on the Columbia River in 1897. MSCUA, University of Washington Libraries, No. UW12691.

At left a boat load of salmon at Ilwaco dock. Below, crab are being unloaded at the Ilwaco dock. The Tribune, *Ilwaco*.

P.J. McGowan Cannery near Chinook on the Columbia River in 1897. MSCUA, University of Washington Libraries, No. UW12682.

A group of men, women, and children gathering razor clams and crab on the beach in 1897. MSCUA, University of Washington Libraries, No. UW12698.

A TOOTHPICK NEAR LONG BEACH. WASH

Loggers cutting down a large tree on the peninsula during the early days.

Cooking Dungeness crab for a meal in 1897. MSCUA, University of Washington Libraries, No. UW12701.

47 Ft. Whale ashore near Breakers
Aug. 18 - 1913

This 47-foot whale that came aground near the Breakers Hotel was of great interest to tourists in 1913. This man is advertising his business, the Kendall Auto Co. Auto Tours. Excursions were conducted via vehicle and horse-drawn wagon.

The wreck of the Admiral Benson, *sinking into the sands near Peacock Spit in 1930.*

The wreck of the Arrow, *taken the first day while lifeboats were still on the ship. The 1947 Urban Collection.*

The fishing troller Troy, *which came aground August 1946. The* Troy *was only the second boat ever removed from a weather beach. Urban Collection.*

Shipwrecks continue to occur in this area of the "Graveyard of the Pacific." Urban Collection.

Cooks preparing the pan for a giant clam fritter to be cooked in the "World's Largest Frying Pan" during the 1941 Clam Festival. The Tribune, Ilwaco.

A 1923 advertisement for Long Beach, "The World's Speedway."

Waikiki Beach just north of Cape Disappointment and east of the jetty in 1973. This is a popular place to swim in the summer. Urban Collection.

The 1910 interior of the Crystal Baths in Long Beach. Note the warning, "Do Not Spit in the Water."

The Peninsula bicentennial celebration held in Oysterville in 1976. The Tribune, *Ilwaco.*

Veteran's of Foreign Wars carrying the colors in the Loyalty Day Parade in Long Beach. Urban Collection.

One of the interesting sand sculptures from the Sandsations festival in Long Beach. Urban Collection.

Chapter Four

EARLY DEVELOPMENT
OF THE PENINSULA

In the early development of the Long Beach Peninsula a major focus was placed on tourism and the natural resource industries of the area. Steamers and ferries brought people, both tourists and settlers, to the peninsula. The railroad and local stages carried these people to their destinations to and along the peninsula with their travel dictated by the tides. During low tides, steamers could not reach the docks and during high tides, stages found it difficult to maneuver on the ocean beach. As time went on, ferries and roads made it easier and more comfortable to travel to and around the area.

Stage Lines, Steamers, and Ferries

In the early days, the easiest way to travel to Oysterville from Ilwaco was to portage between the Columbia River and Shoalwater (Willapa) Bay. One could then travel by boat up to Oysterville. Eventually people like Isaac Whealdon, Jonathan Stout, and Lewis Loomis provided horse-drawn stage and wagon transportation over the beach. When Lewis Loomis bought out Jonathan Stout's stage service he ran four to five teams a day from Ilwaco to Oysterville.

In the summers, thousands of people came from Portland by boat either directly or through Astoria, then transferred to the train or horse-drawn transportation, to complete their trip up the peninsula. One of those boats was the *U.S. Grant.*

The *U.S. Grant,* a small steamer built in 1865, carried freight and passengers across the Columbia River from Astoria to Baker's Bay. Around 1869, Captain John Gray obtained a contract to carry mail and supplies to Fort Canby from Fort Stevens in Oregon. The small steamer also carried mail and oysters from Willapa Bay to Astoria.

When the *Grant* brought passengers into Baker's Bay, the people would be lowered into a small boat and rowed to shore. In the 1870s, Jonathan Stout ran his stage line three times a week to meet the boat. Since there was no dock, he had to back his stage into the water so passengers could climb from the small boat to the stage and not get their feet wet. Eventually a wharf was built that allowed the large boats to dock, which solved the problem of landing passengers and freight.

In order to build a wharf in Ilwaco, a group of businessmen headed by Lewis Loomis formed the Ilwaco Wharf Company. This group sold shares of stock for $50 each until they had gathered $2,500. Soon a wharf was built in Baker's Bay.

Lewis Loomis and his brother Edwin purchased the stage line from Jonathan Stout. They began to run the stage every day between Ilwaco, where they connected with the *U.S. Grant*, and Oysterville. They ran the stage along the beach during low tide. This was a dangerous route and several times during storms the stage and horses were hit by large waves as they traveled. From the beach to Oysterville the stage followed a rugged road cut through the brush and trees. This was a rough ride because the early stages had no springs. The trip between Ilwaco and Oysterville took two separate teams of horses. The original team of four started out from Ilwaco and went as far as Loomis's ranch. At that point, a new team was attached to the stage and it continued on to Oysterville. This same change was made on the return trip.

During this time, the *U.S. Grant* was the only commercial connection between Astoria and the peninsula. On December 19, 1871, the steamer was blown adrift during a storm while anchored at the wharf at Fort Canby. The *Grant* was pushed by the wind and waves onto Sand Island where it was gravely damaged and eventually torn apart by the wind and waves. The captain, J.H.D. Gray, and his brother escaped in a small lifeboat. They had to spend the night in the boat, tossed about by the storm, until they were found and brought ashore in the morning, cold and soaked, but still alive. The *U.S. Grant*, however, was a total loss.

In 1875, Lewis Loomis, Captain J.H.D. Gray, Jacob Kamm, Henry Gile, and John Goulter formed the Ilwaco Steam Navigation Company. In order to replace the *U.S. Grant* they had to sell shares of stock. Five hundred shares, again at $50 each, were sold with a total income of $25,000, which enabled them to purchase the steamer *General Canby*. The *General Canby* arrived in Ilwaco to much fanfare and was immediately put to work carrying freight, passengers, and eventually mail between Astoria and Ilwaco. The Ilwaco Steam

Navigation Company held the mail contract as well as a contract with the Department of the Army to transport men and supplies between Fort Stevens in Oregon and Fort Canby.

One of the largest steamers to travel to the peninsula was the *T.J. Potter.* The *Potter* was a side-wheeled steamer built by the Oregon Railroad and Navigation Company to transport passengers between Portland and Megler. The capacity of the steamer was approximately 650 passengers. During the summer, when transportation to the peninsula was at its peak, additional trains were added to the main line in order to accommodate the larger crowds. The *T.J. Potter* ran between Portland and Megler until 1916. By then the railroad service was declining and within four years, ferry service was bringing both passengers and automobiles into the area.

Some of the steamers were used for excursions around Willapa Bay. In 1922, Captain A.W. Reed of the steamer *Shamrock* announced that he would run his excursions on Sunday from Raymond and South Bend to Tokeland and Nahcotta. He set the schedule to connect with the Ilwaco Railroad train so that those wishing to make connections to Astoria could do so. A round trip fare from Raymond to Nahcotta was $2.

Ferry service to the peninsula began in 1920 through the efforts of Captain Fritz Elfving. He began offering service to vehicles and passengers with a large scow. The scow, loaded with passengers and a few cars, went back and forth between Astoria and McGowan. Captain Elfving did so well with his small improvised ferry that in 1921 he incorporated under the name Astoria-McGowan Ferry Company. That same year he purchased a proper, though small, ferry named *Tourist.* This new boat allowed him to carry more vehicles and passengers in greater comfort.

Also in 1921, Pacific County built a road from McGowan to Chinook to allow vehicles to access the peninsula with greater ease. A road trestle had to be built around Chinook Point, over the water, in order for vehicles to get around Fort Columbia. One can still see some of the pilings today. At that time Elfving docked his ferry at the end of McGowan's Cannery dock on the Washington side and at a dock in downtown Astoria on the Oregon side of the Columbia River.

Eventually, in 1924, Elfving had so much business due to the increase in tourism to the peninsula that he needed a second ferry. He arranged to have the *Tourist No. 2* built and added it to his Astoria-McGowan run. While the first *Tourist* could carry 15 cars and 30 passengers, *Tourist No. 2* could carry 22 cars and approximately 250 passengers.

Captain Elfving and his Astoria-McGowan Ferry Company enjoyed a lucrative business until 1927 when the Union Pacific Railroad decided to compete with him for the vehicle and passenger service between Astoria and Washington. The Union Pacific had a ferry built for them in Portland. This ferry, the *North Beach*, had its first run on July 6, 1927. At the end of summer, when the tourist business dropped dramatically, there were not enough paying passengers for both the *North Beach* and Captain Elfving's *Tourists* to make money. By 1930, the Union Pacific made the decision to discontinue both ferry and train service to the peninsula because they continued to lose money on their investment.

The *North Beach* was purchased by Captain Cal E. Stewart under the business name Columbia Transportation Company. With this purchase the true war of the ferries began. The rival captains tried to outdo each other by upgrading their accommodations, changing their schedules to the most advantageous times, and lowering prices.

In 1931, Captain Stewart had his boat remodeled in Astoria to modify the upper deck and rearrange it so it would have an outside promenade that could be used for dancing. He also had a new coat of paint put on the boat. At the same time Captain Elfving was having a new ferry, somewhat predictably named *Tourist No. 3*, constructed in Astoria. This boat was designed with three decks, with the upper one to be used as an observation deck.

On March 26, 1931, the remodeled *North Beach* resumed her run between Astoria and Megler, with a new schedule calling for the ferry to run eight trips each day. According to the March 27, 1931 *North Beach Tribune*, the remodeled ferry presented:

> an inviting appearance since her recent changes in construction, with outside promenade decks on both sides and in front and rear with an especially good feature in a glassed in front that permits observation by passengers at the bow with full protection from wind and weather. The inside cabin is ample in room and is seated with comfortable wicker chairs and settees and the lunchroom

accommodations are especially good with 17 stools at the counter. One of the latest models of the General Motors radio entertained passengers while crossing the river.

An advertisement for the *North Beach* claimed it was "one of the finest Coffee Shops afloat—We give you time to eat." The rates at this time for the *North Beach* were 25¢ for passengers and $1 each way for automobiles and their drivers.

The new ferryboat *Tourist No. 3* was launched on July 3, 1931, for a practice run between Astoria and Point Ellis. Captain Elfving offered free rides on the first day to allow people to see his new ferry, which was described in the *North Beach Tribune* as "one of the finest, fastest, and best equipped on the Pacific coast with two main decks and an observation deck above and those making the trip were much impressed. The appointments and the beautiful hardwood finish were especially praised." The cabin interior was of mahogany and the floors and handrails of teakwood. The *Tourist No. 3* held 24 cars and 280 passengers. It could cross the river in 45 minutes. To make his ferry even more appealing, Captain Elfving established a passenger service that operated buses from Astoria via the ferry to the peninsula's main tourist destinations and attractions. The buses transported tourists to and from the peninsula four times a day in the summer. It was about this time that Captain Elfving changed his business name to the Astoria-North Beach Ferry Company.

One popular story of the ferry rivalry says that Cal Stewart, in trying to win the ferry wars over his rival Captain Elfving, had his men drive pilings in front of the ferry landing on the Oregon side of the river. This was accomplished in Astoria late on Sunday night in order to prevent Elfving from landing his ferry the next morning. It was said that Captain Elfving saw the pilings and sped up in order to ram them. When he docked, he came up fighting. The ruckus caused the police to come and they arrested those who had constructed the barrier for working without a permit.

To settle the ferry wars, Captain Elfving bought out the loan on the *North Beach* held by the Union Pacific Railroad. He took over the dock at Megler and merged the ferry companies. In 1946, Captain Elfving finally retired and sold his ferries to Merle Chessman. When Chessman died, the Oregon Highway Department gained control over the ferries and utilized a contract company to run them. The ferries last ran between Astoria and Megler on July 28, 1966. The very next day the Astoria-Megler Bridge was opened to traffic, and it is now the main access point to the peninsula from the south.

Ilwaco Railroad and Navigation Company

The peninsula had a narrow gauge railroad that was built by the Ilwaco Railroad & Navigation Company in 1888 and ran until 1930. This railroad was constructed to provide transportation for tourists, residents, the mail, and goods between Nahcotta and Ilwaco and eventually Megler. The train made many stops and in the early days would even halt en route if you flagged it down. Some of the train stops were Nahcotta, Ocean Park, Klipsan Beach, Loomis, Oceanside, Cranberry, Breakers, Tioga, Long Beach, Saltair, Seaview, Holman, Ilwaco, China, Wallicut, Ellis, Chinook, Fort Columbia, McGowan, and Megler. At one point, it was even advertised that the train stopped in front of every hotel on the peninsula. At this time the hotels relied on the train to deliver their guests.

The Ilwaco railroad had several nicknames: The Clamshell Railroad, Poppa Train, The Railroad that Ran by the Tide, and the Irregular, Rambling, and Never-Get-There Railroad. The name Poppa Train came from the fact that during the summer, families came to the beach to stay for several months. During the week, the men of the family went to work in Portland or other inland cities while the family stayed at the beach, but when the weekend came the men caught the *T.J. Potter* and rode the train back to the beach. Families would wait at the train for "poppa" to come in. The nickname Irregular, Rambling, and Never-Get-There Railroad came from the casual way the rail line was run.

In 1900 the Oregon Railway and Navigation Company, part of the Union Pacific system, took control of the railroad and made many changes to try to improve railroad service. Their improvements included new rail cars, air brakes, and better communications.

The Ilwaco railroad was always available for special excursions, to see a beached whale or for a community picnic or event. Many times there was no charge to take the train to an event. The railroad also assisted with rescues by transporting the Ilwaco Beach (Klipsan Beach) lifesaving crew and their equipment up and down the peninsula where needed to rescue people or respond to a shipwreck. In the September 12, 1930 *North Beach Tribune,* an article cited an incident on the railroad years before. According to the story:

> There was to be a prize fight at Nahcotta. Sol Markham was firing the locomotive and Sol says when the train pulled into Nahcotta here came Bill Brumbach and Fred Rogers sneaking down off the top of the cars wet and cold as a pair of drowned rats. "What you been doin' up there?" said Sol. "Sh Sh," replied Bill, shivering. "We bought our fight tickets in Ilwaco but we didn't have the cash for a train ticket, so we hooked a ride." "Well of all things," roared Sol, "Don't you guys know this is a FREE TRIP to the fight?

At a pioneer picnic held in August of 1930, J.A. Morehead read a paper he wrote describing transportation on the peninsula and the railroad. The paper was printed in the *North Beach Tribune* on August 15, 1930. It was during this time that the railroad was closed by the Union Pacific and put up for sale. This is what Mr. Morehead had to say about the early days on the peninsula:

> The Ilwaco Railroad and Navigation Company built the first four miles of their railroad from Ilwaco to Long Beach in the year 1888 and the next year completed it through to deep water on Shoalwater Bay. As very few now living know of the circumstances leading up to the building of the road it might be of interest to mention some of them at this time. Of course the main object of building the line was to care for the heavy influx of settlers that was pouring into Gray's Harbor and Pacific County during the eighties, but there were other reasons for the establishment of the line at the time it was built. Prior to the time the road was projected the method of travel along the coast was by steamer from Astoria to Ilwaco; by the Loomis stage line, Ilwaco to Oysterville over the ocean beach . . . the bulk of oysters were carried from Bay Center, the main source of supply to the Head of the Bay by sailboats and steamer. From here they were hauled by teams to Ilwaco and on the return trip a large amount of freight was carried. A small steamer also was run from the Head of the Bay to the Shoalwater Bay Mill Company's

plant at Sunshine. An opposition dock had been built at Ilwaco and a tramway was being promoted to connect with the boats running to the Head of the Bay. All this threatened the business of the Loomis stage line as well as that of The Shoalwater Transportation Company, operating on the bay. A move was then made by Mr. Loomis to terminate his stage line at the Head of the Bay near the Fisher place and abandon Oysterville as a terminus of the boat and stage lines. Fisher refused to sell his farm and the project was given up. A railroad was now proposed and the citizens were asked to raise a subsidy to help build it. Some eleven thousand dollars was subscribed and work was begun on the road and four miles of road was completed between Ilwaco and Long Beach in 1888. The stock in the company was nearly all owned by local residents excepting that of John and Thomas Crellin who lived in San Francisco. The board of directors included L.A. Loomis, John R. Goulter, H.S. Gile, R.H. Espy, L.H. Rhoades, and B.A. Seaborg. In securing land for terminal purposes a misunderstanding arose among the directors and Mr. Seaborg withdrew from the board and laid out a town on a site at the proposed terminus, which he called Sealand. On the opposite side of the track the railroad built a rival town which they named Nahcotta, and the fight was on to see which of these towns was to be the metropolis of the northwest. Mr. Seaborg built a steamer, which he named the "Suomi" and placed it on the run between Astoria and Ilwaco in opposition to that of the I.R. & N. Co. He secured the mail contract from Astoria to Sealand carrying the mail by team over the ocean beach with Peter Williamson, now of South Bend, as carrier. A lawsuit between the rivals was compromised and the railroad got the steamer, changing her name to "Ilwaco." They also got two rows of blocks off from Seaborg's town. Jacob Kamm of Portland purchased the stock of Seaborg and was made vice president of the company. The first regular conductor of the new road was a man named Robinson and the first engineer was George Jennings. Charley Burch who had filled all the positions on the stage line from stable boy to stage driver was successively section hand, brakeman, fireman, engineer, and conductor on the railroad. The first equipment consisted of a diminutive passenger car purchased second hand, a few boxcars and some flats. Passenger cars were made by placing benches crosswise on some flat cars and covering them with an awning. As the road flourished, four brand new coaches, the "Loomis," the "Easterbrook," the 'North Beach," and "Combination" were purchased in the east and placed in commission. Under the old management the road was operated in a happy-go-lucky manner, the trains not running on any particular schedule and there was probably not one of the employees that ever saw a book of rules. Traffic was heavy from the start and the employees worked until after night, many times, before the day's work was finished. Excursions of five and six hundred people were not unusual and the usual load of the "T.J. Potter" at the height of the season was two or three hundred people coming to the beach. Oyster shipments on "Frisco Day" would run from two to five hundred sacks daily during the season. The road being operated by local people, there was a tendency among our citizens to feel that they had a sort of proprietorship in it and that they should be consulted in its management. This worked fine as long as the management agreed with the citizens. However they did not always agree. There was a great many passes issued especially about election time, if we voted right on matters in which the railroad was interested. At one time there was a difference between the Ilwaco town council and the management of the railroad in which the editor of the Pacific Journal sided with the council and in consequence his pass was taken up. The editor then got out a schedule and time table which was widely circulated at that time reading as follows:

IRREGULAR, RAMBLING, AND NEVER-GET-THERE RAILROAD

MAKES ALL POINTS ON THE PENINSULA BETWEEN

Ilwaco and Nahcotta
Some time during the day unless unavoidably detained by running off the track.

—: TIME TABLE :—

Train Leaves

Ilwaco Dock   When it gets ready

Arrives At

Nahcotta   When it gets there

PASSENGER ACCOMODATIONS

Any gentleman wishing to shoot snipe along the beach or to fish
for trout in the various lakes can do so by notifying the engineer.
Or
Any lady desiring to visit a few minutes at any place en route,
can do so by notifying the president, who will always be found
on the train

THEIR ELEGANT STEAM TUB

Leaves Astoria every day that she can escape the eagle eye of the
inspectors. Passengers are required to furnish themselves with life
preservers, and to take their own risk, also a pair of stilts in case of
low water on the spit.

Connections with the Train at the Ilwaco Wharf Not Guaranteed.

Fare —All they can get
Freight Rates— — — — — — — — — — — — — — — — — —Value of the package

For terms – Apply to the President

Notice – A spotter is employed on every train to prevent beach visitors from
Being robbed by the Ilwaco councilmen and attorney while en route through
The city. Keep on the train and no danger need be apprehended from this
Source. Passengers persisting in alighting in Ilwaco do so at their own risk.

Early Development of the Peninsula

The controversy between the Ilwaco City Council and the Oregon-Washington Railroad and Navigation Company was over the railroad's use of the tidelands. The Ilwaco City Council felt that the railroad dock was an extension of its streets and they had control over the docks. The issue went to court and the court ruled in favor of the railroad because the dock had been built years prior to the incorporation of the town.

In his speech, J.A. Morehead also stated:

> In 1900 the O.W.R. & N. Co purchased the road and later on extended it to Megler, ran the trains on a schedule and placed brass buttons on the employees. The fact that they had their little troubles with the public as well as the old management is evidenced by a clipping from the Ilwaco Tribune of September 1914, edited by the late Charles Gant. Charley did not like the building which had been maintained as a depot at Ilwaco and he did not hesitate to say a few things about the railroad in one of his many noted rhymes:

The Peninsula Pike

By

Charlie L. Gant

There's a railroad they call the Peninsula Pike
Go get me the Bible and read it—
Just two streaks of rust on the top of a dyke-
O, where is salvation? I need it.
From Megler, this railroad goes winding about,
Like two streaks of rust in an alley,
On low joints and high joints we'er jostled about,
'Till the doctor can scarce make us rally.

From Megler to Holman there's 900 pains,
To scourge your anatomy's function.
In fact those who ride are near void of their brains
When they get down to Ilwaco Junction.
You ache in your feet and you ache in your legs,

THE LONG BEACH PENINSULA

You ache in your arms and your shoulders,
In fact one can scarcely stand up on his pegs
As he bounds over split logs and boulders.

There is no place to stop when you wait for a train,
If raining, if sunshine or storming,
If chilled to the core you may struggle in vain
You'll surely find no way of warming.
It's the hen wallow shuffle you get every mile,
The half Nelson hold and the strangle;
And agony lurks where there should be a smile
And the trip is a terrible wrangle.

This railroad was built just after the flood
No effort's been made to improve it—
Just two streaks of rust in the weeds and the mud,
And nothing, it seems, will behoove it.
Thousands of ties nearly rotten today.
Bridges unsafe as the devil.
The rails they were good when first rolled –so they say–
But the road bed is not on the level . . .

You ache in your shoulders and ache in your hips-
Repent of your sins if you travel–
You'll need your Redeemer on one of these trips
Where Old Death is wielding the gavel.
Are you weary of life? Of toil and of strife?
Are you anxious to heavenward hike?
If so you can quickly get rid of your life–
Just take the Peninsula Pike.

Morehead continued:

An article on the same page of the forementioned rhyme notes
that state and road officials inspected the railroad and the official

inspection noted that things are in "first class shape." I wonder if
that is what the people on the Peninsula thought?

After Gant's rhyme was printed in the *Tribune* several improvements were
made to the railroad, including a new depot in Ilwaco.

In 1900, the Oregon Railroad and Navigation Company gained control of
the Ilwaco Railroad and Navigation Company. It revamped the *T.J. Potter* in
1902, adding 40 more overnight rooms, new carpet and furniture, a new hull,
and boiler. The *Potter* was now able to travel 20 miles per hour on the river
between Portland and Ilwaco.

These improvements were able to bring in more tourists and also led
to great improvements in the rail line and facilities. In 1907, a tunnel was
built under Fort Columbia at Chinook Point. This was the last barrier to
extend the line to Megler where there was deeper water and the steamboats
could land during any tide. In 1908 the line was completed, extending the
railroad to Megler.

During the history of the railroad there were many steamers and boats
that provided connections between outside points and the railroad. Some of
them were: the *Nahcotta, General Canby, General Garfield, General Miles, Ilwaco,
Iris,* and others.

On September 9, 1931, the last train traveled the peninsula. On this day
businesses shut down, schools were let out, and people stopped what they
were doing to see the last run of the Ilwaco railroad. When the train reached
the town of Ilwaco, the mayor and other dignitaries made speeches, Charles
Saari played taps on this bugle, and Ken Inman and his crew shot off an old
cannon. Finally, the train blew its final whistle to say good-bye to the crew of
the railroad and an era.

From 1888 to 1931, the Ilwaco railroad traveled up and down the
peninsula carrying passengers and freight. The demise of the train was
mainly due to the increased use of the automobile and the improvement
of roads in the area. It became much more fashionable and convenient to
drive your own car to the peninsula than to travel by boat and train to
your destination.

Chapter Five

NATURAL RESOURCE INDUSTRIES

OF THE PENINSULA

Natural resources and tourism are the economic bases of the peninsula's economy. Industries such as fishing, oystering, crabbing, clamming, logging, and cranberries were major employers in the area.

Oysters

One of the oldest industries on the Long Beach Peninsula is oysters, which were harvested for food and used for trade by the Native Americans long before white men began to explore the Northwest.

Charles J.W. Russell is noted as the man responsible for transporting the Shoalwater Bay oysters to San Francisco markets. He acquired financing to ship oysters and believed if he could find a way to get them to San Francisco before they spoiled, he could establish a lucrative oyster market. Oysters were eventually transported on ice down the coastline to San Francisco by schooner, and the industry took off. As soon as a schooner was docked, individual pickers began to gather oysters. The pickers filled small boats with up to 400 bushels of oysters, with each bushel weighing about 45 pounds. Oysters were then transferred into sacks with two bushels in each sack. The oystermen were paid between 75¢ to $1 per bushel picked.

When the schooner was loaded with 500 to 1,000 sacks, she began her voyage back to San Francisco. Oysters were shipped in the shell until early 1900, after which time they were shucked and iced first, then shipped.

During low tides, oysters would be picked by hand. Tools called tongs were used when the oysters were under water, or during high tide. Tongs were from 6 feet to 12 feet long and resembled two rakes facing each other forming a small basket. When the handles were closed, the basket was opened, and oysters were raked into it. The handles were then pulled apart, the tong pulled out of the water over a boat, and the handles pushed together, releasing the oysters into the boat. Bateaux, flat-bottomed boats about 20 feet long and 10 feet wide, were often used to collect the oysters.

With the increase in schooners arriving at Oysterville to transport oysters, and with no thought toward conservation, the supply began to decrease. Weather also affected the oyster population. The exposed native species were susceptible to damage or death by the freezing temperatures that occurred during low tides. Flooding brought too much fresh water into the bay, causing the eel grass to grow tall and thick. The oyster boats could not get through these patches of grass, and the grass smothered the oysters.

In an effort to revitalize the industry, East Coast oyster seed was brought overland to Willapa Bay. It was found to thrive, and by 1902 oysters were again successfully being harvested on the peninsula. By 1913, East Coast oyster farmers began to experience failures producing their oysters. Because of this, East Coast oyster seed became unavailable for the production of new oysters on Willapa Bay. The already transplanted East Coast variety, however, had continued to grow in Willapa Bay, and the West Coast oystermen continued to harvest them successfully until the summer of 1919. At that time something began to kill the oysters. It was later thought that a red tide was responsible for the destruction. Many oystermen lost everything, including their land, to taxes.

The only other area in the world that raised oysters was Japan. A group of local oystermen were interested in reviving the industry in 1929, so they arranged to have Japanese oyster seed brought to Willapa Bay. The Japanese oyster seed began to grow successfully in the bay and the industry was once again revived.

Oysters spawn in July or August when eggs and sperm are discharged into the water, where fertilization takes place. The tiny larvae are pushed around by the currents, leaving them at the mercy of the tides. They eventually develop into microscopic oysters called "spat." Because the tiny spat may be swept out to sea by the tidal currents, oystermen arrange for them to settle on "cultch," a material used as a base for the larvae to attach itself. The oystermen place dry oyster shells in the bay in the path of tidal currents. These shells are placed into nylon net bags, strung on wires, or scattered on the existing oyster beds, to allow the spat a place to "set." The spat sink down through the water and attach themselves to these solid objects in their path and after four months, the young oysters' shells harden and they are removed from the racks of wire or nylon bags. If too many spat are attached to the same shell, the shell is broken into several pieces. This allows each individual oyster room to grow. They are are then moved to an oyster bed where they continue to mature. Most oysters are harvested at the end of their third year.

Oyster station houses were built out in the bay to house the oyster-workers. A family might live in part of the house, while single workers lived in the other. Those who lived in the oyster station house also kept guard over the oyster beds, so anyone who might want to steal the oysters would be discouraged. Oysters were also brought to the oyster station and transferred to barges to be taken to the cannery or processed for shipping.

Today, oysters are sold fresh, canned, smoked, or as stew. Some that are sold fresh are done so in the shell or shucked. To shuck an oyster, workers use a long knife to open them up. The knife is inserted between the valves in such a manner as to cut the large adductor muscle, which causes the shell to close. The oysters are washed to remove any fragments of shell or other debris and then graded for size and placed in containers for shipment. Since oysters are perishable, they are kept refrigerated.

If the oysters are to be canned, they are given a shot of steam, which kills them and causes their shells to open so they can be easily removed. After the oysters are removed from their shells, they are washed, graded by size, and packed into sterile cans.

Oysters that are smoked are shucked, washed, and placed into a shallow tray. They are smoked by burning hardwood such as apple or alder.

During various types of processing, after the oysters are shucked their shells are put into piles. These shells are mostly used for cultch to catch more oyster spat, but oyster shells have also been used for roads, fertilizer, and the production of lime, art, and novelty goods. Near the canneries, large hills of oyster shells can usually be seen.

Most of the beds are privately owned and it is illegal to remove oysters from them, but there is a small bed near the Washington State Department of Fisheries and Wildlife Willapa Bay field office where visitors can gather oysters.

Oysters come in many sizes and are sold near the oyster beds in small markets to both consumers and restaurants. There are a variety of ways to enjoy them, including raw. Another popular method is to bake them until the shells pop open and dress them with butter and lemon juice. Oyster stew, which generally uses small, canned oysters, is also popular:

Shoalwater Bay Oyster Stew

Open a can of oysters. Small oysters work best.
Dump the can of oysters including the juice into a saucepan.
Add milk or half and half to the oysters. The total of the milk
   or half and half should equal the contents of the container
   of oysters.
Add butter, salt, and pepper to taste.
Heat through, stirring constantly so not to burn.
Do not boil.
Spoon whole oysters into bowl, then pour in the liquid.
Oyster stew is especially good when served with crackers or
   fresh baked bread.
Enjoy!

Cranberries

The Long Beach Peninsula has over 350 acres of cranberries, which is more than one quarter of the cranberry acreage in the entire state of Washington. Anthony Chabot first introduced cranberries to the area. Since he did not live here, Chabot hired a local resident to care for his cranberry vines. The caretaker did not perform in a satisfactory manner, so he was dismissed and Robert Chabot, a nephew of Anthony, was sent to the peninsula to care for his uncle's bog.

The cranberry vines used to create the first bogs on the peninsula in the late 1890s were shipped from Cape Cod, Massachusetts. Chabot's cranberries were harvested yearly by a number of different individuals until 1904, after which time the bogs were abandoned. Because they were not properly cared for, weeds developed and cranberries ceased to be a commercial crop on the peninsula. Lack of transportation, a short growing season, the significant investment needed to get a bog going, and the infestation of pests on the vines increased the problems of raising cranberries commercially. Loss of revenue drove many farmers out of the business by 1917.

In 1923, Washington State University sent D.J. Crowley to the Long Beach Peninsula to help farmers with their cranberry growing problems. Crowley significantly helped the farmers by developing chemical sprays to rid the vines from pests and weeds, and he developed a sprinkler system to protect the cranberries from frost.

But Crowley's ideas cost the cranberry farmers money, and during this time few could afford the materials and equipment needed to help their situation. During the Depression, those who were not serious about cranberry farming were in a position to lose everything, so most of them quit. Those who were serious about cranberry farming somehow survived.

Methods of harvesting the cranberry evolved from hand picking to scooping, vacuuming, and finally flooding. Harvesting by hand was the most time consuming of all the methods: strings were run down the field three feet apart to outline picking rows and ensure all pickers were able to gather all the cranberries in their area. Hand picking was very painful, and often pickers taped the ends of their fingers to protect them from the sharp vines. The hand-harvested cranberries were put in picker boxes. At one time pickers were given a tag or token for each box filled, which could be redeemed at many of the merchants in town. The bog owners then reimbursed the merchants for the tokens that they had accepted.

Scooping was another method of harvesting. The scoops had long handles, with prongs at the end that were driven into the vines, which pushed the cranberries off the vine and into the bottom of the scoop. While easier on the pickers' hands, this method also proved very slow and also caused damage to the vines and bruised the cranberries.

The vacuum method was developed to suck the berries off the vines. While less stressful to the vines themselves, this also was found to not be very successful because it was slow and still bruised the fruit.

Since the 1940s, cranberries have been harvested by a wet method. The fields are flooded and a beater removes the berries from the vines. This causes them to float to the top of the water, where they are easily gathered. Early beaters were pushed along in much the same way as a lawn mower, but later styles were ridden around the bogs.

THE LONG BEACH PENINSULA

After flooding and beating, the cranberries are moved to the corner of the field and confined in one area. The berries are guided onto conveyer belts, which load them into wooden boxes called totes. The totes are transported by truck from the fields to an area where the cranberries are cleaned and sorted. These processed berries are then shipped to frozen storage.

The largest cranberry farm in the Northwest and the largest one-man cranberry farm in the United States in 1946 was Cranguyma Farms, established by Guy Meyers. At that time the farm had 80 acres of cranberries and six acres of blueberries.

Since cranberry demand has traditionally been highest at Thanksgiving and Christmas, other means of marketing have become necessary in order to ensure a more profitable harvest. Many of the cranberries are now converted to juice, but other products include dried cranberries and gourmet sauces. Many diverse products have been developed to help encourage customers to eat cranberries all year round. Thanks to these efforts, the cranberry industry of the Long Beach Peninsula still contributes to the economic diversity of the area.

The Coastal Washington Research and Extension Station was developed in 1923 as a joint project of Washington State University and the U.S. Department of Agriculture. The station carries out research on all aspects of cranberries and gives technical advice to cranberry farmers.

Every year during harvest time in October, a cranberry festival is held on the peninsula. Food, arts and crafts, music, and tours of cranberry bogs are popular attractions during the festival. Demonstrations of how cranberries are harvested are given, and individuals are available to answer questions about cranberries. Even a museum has been developed to explain the processes of cranberry farming, both in the past and present.

Pacific Cranberry Conserve

| 2 quarts raw cranberries | 1 cup diced orange pulp |
| 1/2 pound of raisins | 6 cups of sugar |

Wash cranberries. Cover fruit with water. Cook until berries are soft and pop. Add raisins, sugar, and orange pulp. Simmer slowly until thickened. Put in a bowl and refrigerate until cool.

Fishing

The fishing industry was essential to both the Chinook Indians and to the later settlers of the Long Beach Peninsula. It was very important as a source of food and for the economic stability of the area. Throughout history many types of fishing have taken place in the waters surrounding the peninsula, with gillnetting, trapping, seining, trolling, and sport fishing the most popular types in both the river and the Pacific.

Gillnetting was prevalent in this area in the 1800s. The first gillnet boats were sail powered and measured about 25 feet long, 6 feet wide, and 2.5 feet deep. The mast for the sail was 16 feet high.

A net, as long as 1,400 feet and as deep as 25 feet, was dropped into the water from the gillnet boat. The early gillnetter fastened floats to the net, which caused the top to float on the surface of the water and the net to remain even with the water level. Weights were attached to the bottom of the net to hold it down. Fish would swim up the river and into the net, where they were caught by their gills in the holes. A trammel net, which was a large mesh net, was placed behind the gill net to catch large fish that escaped the gill net.

The gillnet fishermen worked mostly at night because they claimed the fish had a greater problem seeing in the dark. When the river was high and muddy the fishermen also had an advantage over the fish because of poor visibility in the water.

To harvest the catch, fishermen had to pick each fish out of the net by hand. In the early days, the nets were pulled in by hand, but as new gear was developed, motorized machinery pulled did the work. When fishing ended at 6:00 p.m. on Saturday nights, nets were put in bluestone tanks, sometimes for up to 17 hours or overnight, to cut the slime that gathered on the knots of the nets. Seventeen pounds of bluestone (blue vitriol) were used in one tank. Alternatively, tanbark, made from the bark of oak trees, was added to boiling water and the nets could be treated with this solution. The tanbark turned the nets black, but enabled them to leave the boat without tangling. Some of the fishermen thought that the fish could see the black nets and that tanbark was not as good as the bluestone treatment, so an attempt was made to try to match the net color to the water color, so the fish wouldn't see it.

Some families knitted their nets at home in the winter using flax. From 1880 to 1892, 1,240 gillnetters took half of the total catch of fish caught during that time. From 1930 to 1934, gillnetters continued to take half the catch of salmon, but with only half the number of gillnets previously used.

Another invention, the gas motor, helped the fishermen by replacing the sail as a means of propulsion. This allowed the gillnetters to fish closer to the bar, where the river met the ocean.

Purse seining was another form of fishing in the early years. A fishing vessel called a seiner was equipped with a long rectangular net called a purse seine. This had a weighted bottom edge and a buoyant top held afloat by a cork line. The large net encircled a school of fish to contain it and a small boat or skiff was used to maneuver the free end of the net until a larger boat came around to completely form a circle with the net. At this point, the line that ran along the bottom edge of the net was hauled in, forming the "purse" by closing the bottom of the net. The closed purse prevented the fish from escaping under the net, and they could not get over the floating cork at the top. After the excess net was brought aboard, crowding the fish into a smaller area, they were removed either by dipping them out with a large dip net called a brail, or with fish pumps. Later, power deck winches helped pull in the nets.

In the early years, seine crews included 20 to 40 men and five to seven teams of horses. Fish were caught in the net and pulled ashore by men or horses. The best seining grounds were on Sand Island and Chinook Beach. Seining was most effective when the river was low and at daybreak, with the poorest time to harvest being the early afternoon. Seiners were always in competition with gill-netters and trappers for both fish and fishing areas.

Scandinavian fishermen introduced trapping in the 1800s. Trapping was long a successful means of fishing in Scandinavia, and they felt it was worth a try on the peninsula. Fish traps were built along Baker's Bay and the Columbia River, and a successful fishing venture was initiated.

Many traps were built from Baker's Bay to Chinook and the fishing industry boomed. From 1889 to 1892 the number of traps doubled from 164 to 378, but the loss of habitat in the watershed caused salmon runs to decline after 1903. From 1930 to 1934, the number of traps increased but the average catch declined. The gillnetters felt that the traps were catching most of the salmon and leaving only a few for them to catch, since salmon followed the north shore swimming through Baker's Bay, right in the way of the fish traps.

Trolling for salmon became popular once fishermen realized that Chinook and Coho salmon would bite at a baited hook or lure. Several hooks or lures are placed along a long line. As the boat is moving through the water a great number of opportunities are available for the salmon to grab the bait and get hooked. During the Depression hand trolling reached its peak. Trolling poles were added with simple hand cranked affairs, which made it possible for trollers to fish at deeper depths. Trolling was criticized because fish often died from their wounds after they escaped the hooks. Often immature fish were caught and when released they often did not live. There were no trollers between 1889–1892 but after 1892 the number of trollers steadily increased.

Ilwaco has long been the center of sport fishing for the mouth of the Columbia River and the nearby Pacific Ocean area. Sports fishing was not very prevalent during the early days but continually increased and was much more frequent after World War II. Ilwaco had many charter boats and businesses related to these charters located at the docks. Large groups of people would descend on the Peninsula during the fishing seasons filling motels in the area. Eventually, due to increased regulations and fewer salmon, there was a decrease in the number of sports fishermen until the sports fishing industry expanded to include fish other than salmon. The popularity of sport fishing continues today and still draws many tourists to the Long Beach Peninsula.

Clamming

Harvesting razor clams had been both a personal and a commercial venture up through 1968. During the Depression, local residents were able to dig during low tide and sell their clams to buyers for 6¢ a pound. The buyers parked on the beach during low tide in order to be convenient for the clam diggers, who would come along and sell their newly-dug clams. Razor clams are found along the beach close to the water's edge at low tide.

Clams may be successfully dug with a clam shovel or a clam tube/clam gun. The clam reveals its location with a small hole or dent in the wet sand; once it is found, a shovel blade is placed four to six inches on the ocean side of the hole and the blade is pushed straight down. The sand is removed with a twisting action of the shovel, with the clammer making sure the shovel blade remains vertical to avoid cracking the shell. Reaching into the hole to firmly grab the clam is not as easy as it sounds, since it will try to retreat by pushing itself down. The top parts of their shells are also sharp and very dangerous to fingers. Cracked or mutilated clams must be kept and counted as part of the daily bag limit. This industry is now very restricted within the state of Washington and clams may only be dug recreationally during announced seasons and then only with a license.

In 1940 the Town of Long Beach held the first of several annual Clam Festivals. The festival was held for many years and drew thousands of people to the beach.

Crabbing

The crabs that are caught in this area are Dungeness crabs. They have white-tipped claws and a brownish shell. These crabs are harvested commercially in the Pacific just off the peninsula with crab pots that are loaded with bait and dropped by boats into the water. Marking buoys for the crabmens' pots can be seen from the rocks near the mouth of the river. Each crabman has his own buoys that are marked or colored distinctively, showing clearly whose crab pots are below.

The boats return after a number of days, the pots are pulled aboard, and the crabs put on ice. They are brought into the dock and sold to markets or seafood buyers. Many residents and tourists also catch crabs on the peninsula for their own use. This has long been a favorite activity for those who love Dungeness crab.

Canneries

With the number of fish being caught in the 1800s, a method of preserving them became necessary. After the 1820s, the Hudson Bay Company developed a trade in barreled salt salmon. In 1864 William Hume, a fisherman, and Andrew Hapgood, a tinsmith, established a salmon cannery. They were able to preserve and package the fish so it could be sold anywhere in the world. Hume and Hapgood moved their operation to the Columbia River, and in 1867 the canning of salmon began with an output of 18,000 cases. Canned salmon gained importance and by 1869 the output was 100,000 cases, with a market value of nearly $1 million. By 1874, the number of canned fish increased again to 350,000 cases and continued to increase until the number was 650,000 cases in 1884.

One of the first canneries to be built on the Columbia was owned by P.J. McGowan. He constructed his cannery on the beach a mile downriver of the former Hudson Bay Company trading post. The McGowan Cannery was located on the old Stella Maris Mission grant and had a dock extending into the channel, from which boats were sent up and down the river to pick up fish for the cannery. The McGowan Company owned 25 to 30 boats, which along with nets were rented to gillnetters. The fishermen received two thirds of the catch and the company one third, with the boats rented for the season and the rent deducted from the catch of fish. Fishermen had to fish for the company that provided their boats and equipment. The fish were received at the dock and transported on small carts back to the cannery. Many Chinese, as well as workers from the Philippine Islands, worked at the cannery.

The Chinese cannery workers were mostly single men who lived in company housing, mainly in a place called China Hill. They kept to themselves and grew much of their own food in large vegetable gardens near their houses. By 1934, many of the Chinese cannery workers had returned to China, with most of them having made a large amount of money working ten hours a day, six days a week.

When the canneries started to use cans, they made them by a process where the tin was cut into strips with a cutter that was attached to the floor. After the tin was cut it was soldered together to form a can. This was the same method used by Chinese in their own country so it was an efficient and familiar process for them to use. A label made of tissue paper was wrapped around the can and the information and brand name was stamped on the tissue paper.

The canned fish were shipped in wooden cases. It took three Chinook salmon to fill a case of 48 one-pound cans. Each oval-shaped can held three or four slices of fish. Fifty to sixty tons of fish were brought to the McGowan Cannery, and at the end of the season thousands of cases of salmon were towed to Astoria. From Astoria the cases were shipped to various destinations such as New York and San Francisco.

THE LONG BEACH PENINSULA

A small amount of salt was put into the cans, and in 1932 oil was added as well because of the poor grade of the fish. At this time, a crew of female workers did all the packing of cans by hand. The conditions at the cannery were stark and there was little electricity. In 1946, the workers received a pay increase of 25¢, which brought their hourly wage to $1.12. At the same time, the Columbia River Fishermen's Protective Union worked for equal pay for men and women who were doing the same work. After the invention of the mechanical fish cleaner, much of the heavy labor of the cannery was eliminated since the mechanical cleaner could do the work of 60 men. But cannery work today still relies on many hard-working people to process the fish.

According to newspaper accounts, a Columbia River fishermen's strike occurred in 1896 when 4,000 gill-netters threatened to rebel against the fish traps near Ilwaco and Chinook. The fishermen, angry with the cannery men running the traps, decided to settle their grievances personally. The 80-year-old Pacific County Sheriff Tom Roney, commanding the steam launch *Rustler* and its six-inch cannon, came head on with the gillnet fleet. The 63-foot *Rustler* patrolled the waters and a group of 45 men patrolled the shore. The *Rustler* was said to have been Pacific County's first and last warship.

The strike was not an easy matter to settle. It became more serious when a group of fishermen cut fishing gear and dynamited fishing equipment. Traps were destroyed and in one incident strikers moved in on a crew of men driving piling for a new fish trap and set them adrift on their barge near the bar. The barge was heading for the open sea when it was discovered and towed to safety.

Sheriff Roney decided that the strike was too large for him and his men to control, so he and others made a two-day trip to Olympia to urge Governor John H. McGraw to move the militia in to help deal with the violence.

On April 9, 1896, General Eugene Carr, along with 40 officers and enlisted men, left Seattle. Since the Long Beach Peninsula is not easily accessible, the troops traveled overland, came by boat to Nahcotta, and traveled down the peninsula by railway to Ilwaco. Before the fishermen were aware of what was going on, the troops had landed and set up a camp called "Camp Carr" in Ilwaco. The detachment, commanded by Captain Frank E. Adams, continued to patrol the area until July 2, 1896, the end of the fishing season. There was only enough money to fund the troops until that time. During the militia's stay the cannerymen were able to rebuild and continue to operate their traps. But this was not the end of the violence between rival fishing groups. The "fish wars" continued until the traps were prohibited by law in both Washington and Oregon.

Logging

In the late 1800s and early 1900s, logging was a major resource-based industry on the peninsula. In 1912, a major controversy over the logging of timber at Fort Canby and North Head took place. The proceeds of the sale of the timber were to pay for roads between Fort Canby, North Head, and the county road, and also for use by Fort Canby. But the argument was, if the area was logged, no one would want to go there. According to a letter to the editor in the March 16, 1912 *Ilwaco Tribune*:

> However much Ilwaco and all concerned may desire these improvements, to make them at such a cost would be to destroy one of the most attractive features of this whole Peninsula to the people thereof, summer visitors, and world tourists . . . what would anybody want to go to North Head for over any such road.

Proponents of the road felt that it was needed so people would have good access to Fort Canby and the natural areas near the cape. They felt that the trees were dying and needed to be removed anyway, and the money was best spent to improve the roads.

Logging continued on the peninsula, and in 1922 the Parsell and Wilme Logging Company was preparing to log 30 million feet of lumber on Willapa Bay. The company brought in a dredge to deepen the channel at Head of the Bay so the logs could be dumped at that location. The logs were to be towed to the mill in Raymond, and many logs were also transported on the train and taken to Ilwaco to be loaded onto ships.

There was a mill in Ilwaco called the Ilwaco Mill and Lumber Company, located on Baker's Bay and specializing in rough and kiln-dried lumber, sash and doors, moldings, pickets, shingles, and building supplies. They made most of their products from spruce found on or near the peninsula. B.A. Seaborg also had a mill that made boxes, located on Black Lake near the town of Ilwaco. Boxes from his mill were used to ship the cans of salmon from his cannery on Baker's Bay in Ilwaco.

Today a small amount of logging is done to clear land on the peninsula but it is no longer a major industry as it once was. Just off the peninsula toward the east are many tree farms and the logging industry is of major economic interest to the rest of the county. But the Long Beach Peninsula has survived economically because of its variety of natural resource–based industries. Regulations and laws have been enacted over the years to help preserve these resources for future generations.

Chapter Six

THE PENINSULA AS A
TOURIST DESTINATION

The Long Beach Peninsula began to develop as a tourist destination soon after settlement began. Its popularity increased with time, and by the early twentieth century the peninsula was one of the most popular places to visit in the Northwest. Many attractions lured visitors to the area besides the Pacific Ocean beaches. People were drawn to the natural beauty, natural resources, shipwrecks, and festivals. Both simple and extravagant accommodations were available and land was obtainable for those who wished to buy and build a "summer place" or permanent residence. Both salt and fresh water baths were offered for good health and the many curio shops were a delight to bargain hunters. In the early days visitors reached the peninsula by steamer and train. Later, motor vehicles made travel easier.

Shipwrecks

More than 2,000 ships have wrecked and many lives have been lost near the mouth of the Columbia River. From small fishing boats to large sailing ships and freighters, most sank due to the unpredictable wind, waves, shifting sands, and currents in this area known as "the graveyard of the Pacific."

The earliest documented sinking of a ship in this area was the *William and Ann* in 1829. The vessel belonged to the Hudson Bay Company and was carrying general merchandise to Fort Vancouver. The 46 people aboard all perished when she went down.

Although many shipwrecks have occurred here, some stand out in history for their notably unique circumstances. Four of the most notable shipwrecks that happened near the Long Beach Peninsula were the *Peacock*, the *Admiral Benson*, the *Vazlav Vorovsky*, and the *Arrow*.

U.S.S. *Peacock*

The earliest of the four shipwrecks mentioned above was that of the U.S.S. *Peacock*, which wrecked just off Cape Disappointment on July 18, 1841. According to the navy's historical records, the *Peacock* was built in 1813 as a U.S. Naval sloop of war and was later attached to the Wilkes Exploring Expedition for a three-year period, until it was wrecked. The ship's crew and scientists had been exploring and charting the areas around Samoa and the Sandwich Islands (Hawaii).

According to the official navy report of October 30, 1841, by Charles Wilkes, commanding officer of the U.S. Exploration Expedition, the *Peacock* was ordered to leave Oahu on December 2, 1840, and instructed to head for the Columbia River. On July 17, 1841, it reached the mouth of the Columbia River, where Captain William L. Hudson attempted to cross the Columbia River bar with some outdated and inaccurate charts that were given to Lieutenant Charles Wilkes by Captain Spaulding of the ship *Lausanne* at Oahu. Captain Spaulding assured Wilkes that the charts and directions were accurate and could be relied on. Neither captain understood how quickly the sands in the channel changed. With these out of date directions and charts as their guide, the outlook for the *Peacock* was not good.

Due to dense fog, the ship waited until the morning following its arrival off the river mouth to attempt to cross the bar. According to Wilkes's report, "We brought Cape Disappointment to bear NE 1/2E by compass and was heading up to it to bring Cheenook point (Chinook Point) to bear ENE when we discovered the sea breaking ahead of us." The ship turned to clear the breakers and attempted to enter the river where the water was smoother. In so doing, the *Peacock* missed the main channel and hit the sands with so much force it became stuck. The report continued:

> The ship was now lifting and striking heavily and the sea had become too furious. . . . [We] had the pumps rigged, sent the royall and top gallant yards, masts, and rigging on deck, and every thing of weight out of the tops to save our lower masts from switching over the side, finding the ship was now taking water fast, divided the

watches in gangs at the pumps and kept them going from that time until the boats left the ship.

The crew had thrown overboard all the excess rigging and cargo in an attempt to free the ship from the sands. They then threw everything else they could over the side including the cannons, shot, and supplies. The rudder was broken off by the action of the waves and the ship was continuously driven against the sand. The *Peacock* was forced broadside to the waves until it filled with water and there was no choice but to abandon ship. Again from Wilkes's report:

> The ship at this time striking so heavily that I had little hopes of her holding together till daylight . . . at 7 a.m. of the 19th the first opportunity which occurred when a boat could be ventured over the side or reach the shore, Lt Perry was dispatched with the charts papers and everything connected with the surveys of the present cruise, Purser Speiden with his books and accounts—The Launch and three boats hoisted out, some trifling provisions put in the former, and all the boats of the ship successfully filled with the crew officers and scientific gentlemen, the Marines only taking their arms and accoutrements, and no one allowed to take any clothing but what they stood in."

Captain Hudson, Lieutenant Walker, Boatswain Carpenter, and Purser Steward had remained on the ship. When the water rose even higher on the deck, they cut the masts in the hope that it would help the ship stay together long enough for the boats to come back and remove them. It was just before sunset on July 19 that the four were rescued and taken to where the other survivors had landed on Baker's Bay. The report further stated:

> We found brush huts erected, fires burning and the gentlemen of the Methodist Mission Mesr Frost & Kone and Mr. Birnie agent of the Hudson Bay Coompany from Fort George with provisions for our relief, all that has been saved from the ship are the charts made during the cruise, the work of the surveys, some few journals of

the Scientific gentlemen and officers, with the Purser's books and accounts the chronometers and all the boats with the exception of the first cutter.

No lives were lost in the sinking of the *Peacock*, but the ship was broken apart by the pounding of the waves and could not be rescued. It was noted that only the bowsprit was visible by the next day and even that eventually disappeared. The sands that were the cause of the ship's demise were accordingly named "Peacock Spit," a name they retain today.

S.S. *Admiral Benson*

On February 15, 1930, the steamship *Admiral Benson* lost its bearings at the mouth of the Columbia River, missed the main channel, and became grounded near the end of the North Jetty. The *Benson* was stuck just yards from the wreck of the American freighter *Laurel*, which sank there in 1929. The sight of the *Laurel's* mast must have been a sad reminder of that earlier wreck, which had claimed the life of a young sailor. The *Benson* was carrying 39 passengers and 65 crewmembers along with a load of fruit and freight headed upriver for Portland.

It was evening, just a little before 7 p.m., and the weather was both stormy and foggy when she went aground. At first Captain C.C. Graham thought he could back the steamship off the sands so he did not send out a distress call, just a request for assistance. Coast Guard crews from both Point Adams and Cape Disappointment and the freighter *Nevada* responded to help evacuate passengers and crew if needed.

The Coast Guard used a Lyle gun to shoot a line to the ship and establish an evacuation route for passengers and crew from the ship to the beach, but most of the passengers and some of the crew were evacuated from the *Admiral Benson* in lifeboats. Those who remained did so with the hope of getting the ship off the sands during high tide. But the weather continued to worsen until the winds reached 70 miles per hour and the action of the wind and the waves eventually began to tear the ship apart. The remaining passengers and more of the crew were removed from the ship.

The next day the rest of the crew was evacuated by breeches buoy to the beach, leaving the captain alone on his ship. But after almost a week, even

Captain Graham gave up on the ship and came ashore. No lives were lost in this incident either, and some of the ship's cargo and equipment was even able to be salvaged before it broke apart and sank into the sands. The beach just to the north of the jetty was named Benson Beach in honor of this ship that wrecked near its sands.

Vazlav Vorovsky

The Russian steamship *Vazlav Vorovsky* ran aground on Peacock Spit just south and east of Cape Disappointment on April 3, 1941. The ship was headed outbound in an attempt to cross the Columbia River bar when a storm came up forcing the ship back into the river. The *Vorovsky* was tossed by the storm, lost her steering, and was forced to drop both its anchors in an attempt to keep from running aground. But the anchors did not hold and the *Vazlav Vorovsky* was pushed onto Peacock Spit.

The U.S. Coast Guard was immediately dispatched in three lifeboats to rescue the crew of 37 men and two women. The crew was loaded into the lifeboats and safely taken to Point Adams Coast Guard Station, but Captain S.J. Tokareff refused to leave his ship. It was not until the next evening, after the ship started breaking up, that the captain requested to be removed from the *Vorovsky*. According to news reports, Tokareff was injured when his leg was crushed between the ship and the lifeboat.

The *Vorovsky* continued to develop large cracks and eventually buckled under the action of the waves and sand. The ship had been carrying a cargo of well drilling machines, tools, wool rags, and lard valued by Lloyds of London in excess of $1 million. The cargo had been picked up in Portland and was headed for Vladivostok, Russia.

Interestingly, much of the lighter cargo eventually floated out from the wreck and washed ashore. Especially notable were the thousands of cases of boxed lard found all over the beach. Much of this was salvaged by area residents, and a crew hired by Lloyds salvaged some of the machinery off the ship. The Russian ship *Vazlav Vorovsky* finally broke apart and slowly disintegrated into the sands of Peacock Spit.

THE LONG BEACH PENINSULA

Arrow

On February 13, 1947, the 320-foot Army transport *Arrow* was being towed by a tugboat from Puget Sound to Tongue Point. The *Arrow* had at one time been a luxury liner called the *Belfast*, built in Maine in 1909. The Army purchased the lavish steamer during World War II, converted it for wartime use, and used it as a ferry in the Hawaiian Islands.

In 1947 as the tug and *Arrow* approached the Columbia River, a storm caused the towing line to break several times. Each time the crew was able to retrieve the line and reattach it, but the last time, it could not be retrieved and the *Arrow* drifted toward the beach. The ship ran aground near Cranberry Road approach and was mercilessly pounded by the surf. The *Arrow* was reported to be "about 50 yards from shore at low tide." Her bow was pointed to the south and for a while the ship was guarded by troops in the hope that it could be salvaged. Eventually it was determined that the *Arrow* was dug into the sand too deep and that it was fast sinking even deeper. The movement of the sand ultimately broke the ship in two. Beachcombers were able to salvage a few items off of the *Arrow*, and as it slowly sank into the sand over the years, it became a favorite place to surf fish.

A few years after the wreck of the *Arrow*, a group of Ocean Park residents removed the masts and mounted them at the entrance of the Ocean Park approach. This was designated as a war memorial and dedicated during a large celebration.

The *Peacock*, *Admiral Benson*, *Vazlov Vorovsky*, and the *Arrow* were but four of the many ships that have wrecked along the Long Beach Peninsula. With their remains along with those of the many other ships wrecked on the beach and rocks buried just offshore, much debris has been washed ashore on the peninsula over the years, leading to sometimes surprising finds for the many beachcombers who walk or drive along the shore.

Beachcombing

One of the most popular activities on the Long Beach Peninsula over the years has been beachcombing. People have found Japanese glass floats of various sizes and shapes while walking on the beach, and it is not uncommon to find parts of ships or unusual cargo that has come ashore. Besides these, cargo such as lard, flour, shoes, and lumber have also been found.

Sometimes unusual sea life from the South Pacific or strangely shaped driftwood is also carried by the currents to the beaches of the peninsula. Two popular buildings, the Wreckage, a house in Ocean Park; and the former Driftwood Hotel in Long Beach, were constructed of driftwood and other items their builders found washed up on the beach.

Activities and Places to Visit

Surf fishing always was and still is a popular pastime on the peninsula. While people have fished most anywhere along the beach, one of the most popular places has been the fishing rocks near Beard's Hollow, where people would travel to picnic and fish off the rocks. The hollow was named for Captain E.N. Beard of the wrecked ship *Vandalia*, which went down in January of 1853 near McKenzie Head. Captain Beard was one of four victims of the shipwreck who washed up on the beach near this hollow.

South of Beard's Hollow is Dead Man's Hollow, named for the many shipwreck victims who have washed up on the beach. Favorite places to visit here were Echo Cave, along with the rocks known as the Harp, Needles, and Sugar Loaf.

The northern part of the peninsula has also traditionally offered activities for the tourists. Peninsula Point or Ledbetter Point, located on the very northern tip, has always been a popular place to see the entrance to Willapa Bay. This was also long a popular place to dig for clams, catch crabs, go for a walk, or picnic.

Two main golf courses were located on the peninsula during the early days. One was the Moby Dick Golf Course, a small course near Nahcotta on the bay, and the other was called Torwoodlea, which was located on the bay near the Peninsula Highway. Torwoodlea opened on Memorial Weekend in 1931 with much festive activity.

During this time, razor clam digging and catching crabs were everyday activities for many people. Large dungeness crabs could be pulled out of holes filled with water left on the beach during the low tide. Clamming was also a low tide activity. While one could dig commercially with a license, for the residents and tourists there were no restrictions except that the canning of clams was not allowed during the summer months. Digging was possible for personal use but none could be put aside for the winter during this time.

Festivals and Events

Over its history the Long Beach Peninsula has hosted numerous festivals and events. Some of the more popular activities have been the Fourth of July, the "Cranberrians Community Fair," Tourist Ball, and the Clam Festival.

The Ilwaco Fourth of July celebration became quite a large event in the early days. In 1912, an advertisement was published that declared the following:

4TH OF JULY

Come and See Us

Going to Have Good Old Time
Celebration at Ilwaco

We Know How to do Things
And Goin' to do'em

Leave Your Squir'l Rifles at Home
But Bring Wife and Daughters
And Visitin' Friends

Everybody on the North Shore from Oysterville to
Frankfort are Coming. They Can't Stay Away

Many other events were scheduled during the Fourth of July celebration, including several sporting events. Events held in Ilwaco were the 100-yard races, 50-yard races, a sack race, high jump, and running broad jump. A horse race, pony race, potato race, and fat man's race were also scheduled. Prizes from $1.50 to $15.00 were given for the first place winners. A baseball game, gasoline fish boat races for different size engines, and a competition for the best decorated automobile were also held, followed by a dance in the evening at the Ilwaco Opera House.

During the 1922 Fourth of July celebration, a Goddess of Liberty contest was held. Voting boxes were placed in many stores around the peninsula so people could vote for the most popular young lady. The votes were sold at 1¢ each, or 110 votes for a dollar. The winning young lady presided over the celebration and activities.

In 1931, the Long Beach celebration of the Fourth of July featured several parades. A clown parade, pajama parade, and pet parade were held along the main street of town, with many taking part. The Fourth of July celebrations were very popular and well attended by tourists and locals alike. Through the years, many spent the evening of the Fourth on the beaches building large bonfires and shooting off fireworks.

In 1922, the Cranberrians Community Fair was held at Sylvan Hall in Long Beach. Many events and exhibits were held in conjunction with the fair. Some of the exhibits included poultry and livestock, garden produce, cooking, and needlework. Prizes were given for the best in each event. In 1923, this fair became the North Beach Cranberrian Fair and in 1931, the name had changed again to just the Cranberrian Fair, which was held at the new grange hall with plans to continue the event permanently there.

For many years a Tourist Ball was held toward the beginning of the tourist season. In 1923, the highlight of this event was the prize waltz, where a prize was given to the best couple dancing the waltz. In 1923, Long Beach also held the first of its auto races on the beach and in 1924 the event grew even larger. These auto races were sponsored by the American Automobile Association. It was said that speeds on the beach reached a high of 80 miles per hour, which was quite fast for the cars of the time. Along with the 60-mile auto race for light and heavy stock cars there were horse races, sack races, pie eating contests, a ladies' nail driving contest, egg race, potato race, and swimming events. A bathing girl's parade, bicycle race, skating race, and a baseball game were also featured. A motorcycle polo match immediately followed the main auto races.

THE LONG BEACH PENINSULA

A lively affair called Days of '49 was sponsored by the Long Beach Chamber of Commerce and held at the new Marsh Amusement Hall in 1931. The *Ilwaco Tribune* on May 29, 1931, reported, "the ladies will dance in their most gay and gaudy beach pajamas and the men will wear red silk shirts with bandana kerchiefs around their leather necks and broad rimmed hats." The event was supposed to simulate the 1849 history of the Pacific coast. The article continued:

> on account of the hard times there will be no gold dust in the pokes but paper currency of "Thousand Buck" denominations will be in use and the boys will play them high at the games of faro, roulette, blackjack, bullfrogs, blandet wheels, and jack rabbits. Between times there will be jitney dancing with the pajama girls and a partaking of the '49 sandwich special, commonly called hot dogs.

The money raised at this event was used on the Grays River–Skamokawa Pioneer road and on peninsula advertising.

In 1940 the Town of Long Beach held its first annual Clam Festival. According to the *Ilwaco Tribune* of May 2, 1941, the 1941 festival drew one of the largest crowds to ever visit the peninsula:

> Not only did it prove a tough task to furnish the chowder and fritters, but the job of feeding the crowd in the eating places was almost too much for the facilities, which were strained to the limit. The attendance from the Washington side of the river was huge and there was a stream of cars on every ferry from Astoria. It was reported that there were strings of cars left behind from lack of capacity to handle them.

The paper estimated that more than 20,000 people came for these events. The locals who served as chefs estimated they served 2,600 cups of clam chowder, but many more people were served by the nine-foot clam fritter that was cooked in the "World's Largest Frying Pan." It reportedly took over 200 pounds of clams, 20 dozen eggs, 20 pounds of flour, 20 pounds of cracker meal, 20 pounds of corn meal, and 10 gallons of milk to make the big clam fritter. A Clam Festival Ball was held in conjunction with the big cooking extravaganza.

In later years, the World's Largest Frying Pan was sent to several cities to advertise the peninsula Clam Festival. In 1947, the pan toured Portland on a truck that advertised the giant fritter that would be cooked in it. Advertisements claimed that pieces of the fritter would be offered for free and served as all-you-can-eat. Clam digging, surf fishing, and bathing beauties were also advertised. The World's Largest Frying Pan is 9 feet 6 inches in diameter and can still be seen at one of the downtown Long Beach mini-parks.

The Long Beach Peninsula Bicentennial Celebration was held in Oysterville on July 4, 1976. The program was sponsored by the Shoalwater Bay Chapter of the Daughters of the Pioneers of Washington state. A formal program, picnic, dance, displays, and horseshoe throwing were held at the Bicentennial Celebration. A pageant was presented depicting the dramatic events when a group of of South Bend citizens broke into the Oysterville County courthouse and stole the county records. In the evening, many peninsula residents attended a dance at Bardheim's barn. It was a time to celebrate the nation's bicentennial and to celebrate Oysterville's historic past.

Chapter Seven

THE PENINSULA TODAY

Many changes have occurred here over the years since Robert Gray and Lewis and Clark first opened the peninsula to European settlement. One of the most significant changes has been the transformation of the Columbia River itself. After the jetties were built, the ocean breakers were not as evident at the mouth of the river. In 1805 Lewis and Clark were temporarily trapped in their "dismal nitch" because of the storm and high waves. That kind of weather would not pose as big a problem if they arrived in the same nitch today, even though the river can still get quite rough. But the jetties have not only caused a change in the Columbia's character, they have led to dramatic physical changes to the landforms as well.

Sand Island has slowly shrunk and shifted toward the west over the years. When the South Jetty was built, the channel moved and the currents and waves came from a different direction. During the days of fish trapping, the majority of the traps were placed near Chinook and Sand Island, when the island was much larger and extended closer to Chinook.

While Sand Island shrank, Peacock Spit has increased to more than 1,000 acres due to the building of the North Jetty. Here the movement of the channel and currents caused the sands to shift and fill in the area to the north of the jetty to a height of approximately 15 feet. Over the years the beach area was built up and land accrued in this area. Now, the jetties are beginning to break down, and the sand in some of the new beach areas is slowly eroding away into the ocean again.

During the days of the railroad, the ocean at high tide came very close to what is now the Boulevard in the town of Long Beach. Today, with the build up of sand, the beach area has accrued much more land. The beach-front property owners used to own title to the land as far down the beach as the high tide mark, but with the new land the question arose as to who owned the extra property. The courts decided each case individually, with some property owners determined to own just to the old high tide mark, while others owned the new land.

Today, the Town of Long Beach manages the land within the town from the boardwalk to the high tide mark, which keeps the beach area open for public use. The hard sand at low tide establishes a state highway on the beach, but drivers need to watch out for buried driftwood and be aware of the incoming tide. Many cars end up stuck when their drivers do not realize that the ocean is coming in around them, or while leaving the beach through the soft sand at the beach approaches.

Over the years many of the coastal landforms have changed, and due to the influences of the waves, currents, and wind they will continue to change regardless of human development. The breakdown of the jetties is hastening this process, just as their construction did before in 1895 and 1917. No doubt many locals' and visitors' images of the coastline have already changed from what they knew years ago, and will continue to change in the future.

While the landscape changes, much of the peninsula's history has been preserved. For those who are interested in the history of the area, many historical sites offer interpretations of the past. One such site is Fort Columbia, two miles east of Chinook. Fort Columbia offers a view of the peninsula's military heritage, with many of its original buildings still intact. One of the officer's houses, "Commander's House," displays artifacts of the Victorian era from the late 1800s and early 1900s.

The Fort Columbia museum is located in the main barracks where the history of coastal defense at the mouth of the Columbia River is interpreted. An excellent Chinook Indian exhibit is located on the second floor. Rooms such as the kitchen, dining room, sergeant's office, and bunkroom are depicted as they would have been during the World War I era. Bunkers, gun sites, and river overlooks can all be found on the grounds, with trails branching out from the main site of the fort and leading to observation areas and bunkers.

The Peninsula Today

Two houses, the Steward's House and the Scarborough House, may be rented overnight. The Steward's House, built in 1902, was the home of the fort's hospital steward. The Scarborough House was also built in 1902 and was the fort's hospital, named in honor of Captain James Scarborough, who was one of the first outside settlers in this area.

In Ilwaco, the Ilwaco Heritage Museum offers displays of the Chinook Indians, the industries of the area, topics of local interest, a railroad exhibit, and a miniature railroad showing where the train ran throughout the peninsula. The old No. 10 train car "Nahcotta" is located next to the museum.

The Colbert House, built in the mid-nineteenth century, is also located in Ilwaco and was placed on the National Register of Historic Places in 1977. The center part of the house was originally built in Chinookville, but when Fred and Catherine Colbert moved their family to Ilwaco in 1883, a short while later they decided to also move their house. It was disassembled in Chinookville, loaded onto a barge, and towed to Ilwaco. There it was reassembled at its present location.

As the Colbert family grew, more rooms were added to the house. In 1891 Colbert added a parlor, porch, and bedroom. In 1896, another addition containing a dining room, kitchen, pantry, and a large workroom was constructed. Colbert was a very successful businessman in the area: in Chinookville he had seined for salmon, but after he moved to Ilwaco he began to use fish traps. Later he opened a livery and delivered goods to customers throughout the area. Soon after, Colbert was appointed postmaster and also elected justice of the peace. His house was restored in 1994 with much attention to detail and now provides a good example of how people of that time lived. Colbert family artifacts were used to help furnish the house, which is located on the corner on Quaker Street between Spruce and Lake in Ilwaco and is maintained by Washington State Parks as a museum.

Just west of Ilwaco, Fort Canby today features a campground, the Lewis and Clark Interpretive Center, access to the North Jetty, many trails, and a boat launch. Two miles of ocean beach, called Benson Beach, and over six miles of hiking trails offer opportunities to explore the area. The North Jetty is accessible for much of its length and is a popular spot for fishing and viewing vessels crossing the Columbia River bar. From Benson Beach, Cape Disappointment lighthouse, the Lewis and Clark Interpretive Center, North Head Lighthouse, the North Jetty, the Columbia River, and the Pacific Ocean can all be viewed.

The Lewis and Clark Interpretive Center holds and interprets many aspects of the peninsula's history. The interpretive center also has the most amazing view of where the Columbia River meets the Pacific Ocean. Inside, from large windows, one can whale watch, view ships going over the bar, see the North Jetty, Fort Canby State Park, and many birds flying past.

The center's main purpose however is to present the journey of Lewis and Clark as they made their way west. The center has recently been remodeled and new exhibits installed, including photographs, artifacts, and a movie. One section of the interpretive center features a maritime theme. The Fresnel light taken from North Head lighthouse is displayed along with a life-saving boat and maritime rescue equipment. Outside the center is an area from which large disappearing guns were placed during World War II, when bunkers were built in the hillside in many locations along the coast. Battery Harvey Allen is one example that can be visited from the interpretive center site. Another can be seen by walking the trail up McKenzie Head.

The lighthouse at Cape Disappointment is located to the south of the Lewis and Clark Interpretive Center. While the light helped coastal navigation, even after it was built shipwrecks continued because ships traveling from the north could not see Cape Disappointment light until they were dangerously close to the rocks.

To help this situation, North Head light was built two miles north of Cape Disappointment and began operation May 16, 1898. The lighthouse stands 65 feet tall and was designed by German born engineer C.W. Leick. Solid basalt holds the lighthouse in place more than 190 feet above sea level. Three lighthouse keepers once staffed the North Head Lighthouse around the clock, and each keeper had his own living quarters. Views from either of the lighthouses or their grounds are equally spectacular. In the summer, tours of North Head lighthouse are available and the original lighthouse keeper's residence now can be rented overnight from Washington State Parks.

Other sites under the management of the Washington State Parks and Recreation Commission include Pacific Pines, Loomis Lake, and Leadbetter Point. Pacific Pines is about one mile north of Ocean Park on the ocean beach and has an access to the beach. Loomis Lake, located four miles south of Ocean Park, is a freshwater lake ideal for fishing from the dock or a boat. Leadbetter Point is the northern most point of the Long Beach Peninsula, and separates Willapa Bay from the Pacific Ocean. It is three miles north of Oysterville and is designated for daytime use only. In 1788, John Meares originally named this dry sandy area "Low Point." It is now closed between March 15 and September 15 to protect the nesting sites of the snowy plover, which has been listed as a threatened species. During this time walkers in the park must stay on the wet sandy areas. Leadbetter Point beach is available for hiking, beach combing, and wildlife observations and is managed by the U.S. Fish and Wildlife Department along with Washington State Parks.

The World Kite Museum, located on 3rd North in Long Beach, displays the history of kites as well as exhibiting many kites from different countries. This museum gives one the motivation to "go fly a kite." With 28 miles of beach along with plenty of space and wind to do so, all the necessary ingredients are available for a fun-filled time.

Marsh's Free Museum is a unique institution located in Long Beach. With unusual items from around the world, including antiques and other interesting objects, Marsh's Museum is a great place to visit. Many of the items on display were gathered over the years from all over the world by Wellington Marsh. Jake the Alligator Man, one of the more unusual items in the museum, is a hit with both young and old. Although commercial in nature, Marsh's does have many museum-quality items visitors can view for free.

The Cranberry Museum, on Pioneer Road in north Long Beach, shares its site with the Washington State University Long Beach Research and Extension Unit. The history of cranberries in this area is interpreted here along with pictures showing how cranberries were harvested in the past and the changes that have taken place in this industry throughout the years. Some of the original harvesting implements are shown within the museum and a film explaining the processes of both wet and dry cranberry harvesting gives viewers an understanding of the methods.

During the Cranberry Festival, tours bring visitors to this site to view first hand how the cranberries are flooded, corralled into one area, and gently pushed onto a conveyor, transferring them into a tote, onto a truck, and finally transported to the plant for processing.

The Willapa Bay Interpretive Center is located in Nahcotta on the bay, and explains the history of the 150-year-old oyster industry. The building, in the form of an oyster station house, offers an interpretation of the oysters and their harvest. Both historic pictures and actual artifacts help in the explanation of this industry. From this location, a view of the bay and the oyster beds are also available. The oyster beds are all privately owned, with the exception of a small area opposite the Washington State Department of Fisheries and Wildlife Willapa Bay field office in Nahcotta.

Three ports are located on the Long Beach Peninsula. The ports at Chinook, Ilwaco, and Nahcotta all offer an opportunity to watch the coming and going of fishing boats. In Nahcotta, oysters are the main industry and oyster barges bring the shellfish in for processing. Here one can watch as the barges are unloaded and the oysters taken to the cannery for processing. Conveyer belts remove the oyster shells from the cannery and drop them onto trucks, to be hauled away. Large mounds of oyster shells can always be seen near the canneries. These shells will be used for cultch for the oyster beds, and for other products.

Other interesting activities include the many local festivals such as the Loyalty Day celebration in May, which provides citizens an opportunity to show their loyalty to the United States and its armed forces. This celebration was first developed by the local Veterans of Foreign Wars Post 3721. The observance includes a parade with local and neighboring areas sending bands and floats. Military units participate in the parade, including veterans from past wars who are honored and invited to walk or ride in the parade. At the conclusion of the parade, a patriotic program of remembrance is held.

The Northwest Garlic Festival is held in Ocean Park in June. It is located at the City Park and school, just off the main highway. Booths feature garlic, garlic products, and garlic crafts that are available for sale. Music, entertainment, games, and food are all geared toward encouraging festival participants to enjoy garlic.

Ocean Park also hosts an Old Fashioned Fourth of July, featuring a parade and festival. Participants come from around the Pacific Northwest to join in this celebration, with spectators lining the street throughout town.

On July 3, at the Port of Ilwaco, a fireworks display is shot off after dark in celebration of Independence Day. On the evening of July 4, another fireworks display is sponsored by the Town of Long Beach. This display takes place on the beach, near the ocean between Bolstad and Sid Snyder Drive.

In July, the festival called SandSations takes place on the peninsula, when groups compete for prizes for the best sand sculptures. Master groups, novice groups, families, and youth divisions work diligently to perfect their unique works of sand art. The sand sculptures stay intact after the festival until the ocean waves fill in the low areas and eventually wash the sculptures away.

In August, Long Beach hosts the week-long Washington State International Kite Festival. During this week, many different types of kites are featured including trains, tubular, Cody, and fighter kites. Music accompanies many of the events, while kites fly and perform stunts to the beat of the songs. Rokkaku kite battles add a bit of excitement to the festival. In these battles, teams fly large kites and try to knock the other team's kites out of the sky or break their opponents' strings. Store-bought, homemade, and professional kites are all welcome, with the variety adding to the lively appearance of the festival. Fireworks are also included as part of the festivities during the weekend of the festival. They take place after a scheduled night flight, featuring several lit-up kites flying high above the crowds to the sounds of music.

The Rod Run to the End of the World, sponsored by the Beach Barons Car Club, is held in September. A car show of antique and classic cars is held at the club's clubhouse off Sandridge Road. Special events related to the cars are also held during this weekend.

THE LONG BEACH PENINSULA

The Annual Cranberrian Fair is held in October at the Ilwaco Heritage Museum, with crafts and cranberry products featured. Local craftsmen sell their homemade items while others are available that show the processes of quilting, rug hooking, and other artistic crafts. Food is available, as well as trolley rides to area cranberry bogs, the Cranberry Museum, and the Cranberry Research Center. The harvesting of cranberries is demonstrated to attendees who take the tour. Music and food are available in the museum, and the museum is open for visitors to see its exhibits about the peninsula area.

Another event that has grown over the years is the Water Music Festival, held on the peninsula at several venues including the Oysterville church, Ilwaco High School, and the Peninsula Church Center. The Water Music Festival Society was founded to provide great performers a stage for their talents in Southwest Washington. The society began in 1985 and continues to offer a variety of music performed by master performers. From opera to jazz, musical artists entertain and work with students interested in the craft of music and the whole community has the opportunity to be exposed to great music through this festival.

"Ocian in View" is a cultural and historic enrichment program about Lewis and Clark's journey to the Pacific Ocean. This program has been held for the past couple years to help make people aware of the upcoming bicentennial of Lewis and Clark's journey to the lower Columbia area. Tours have been offered to interpret the days Lewis and Clark spent along the Columbia River in the final days of their trek to the Pacific Ocean. Various programs have been presented, including oral history interpretations of various members of the Lewis and Clark expedition, along with topics of interest from this period. This enrichment opportunity offers the participants a varied and interesting interpretation of this historical event.

Other special festivals and activities include the Ragtime Rhodie Dixieland Jazz, the NPRA Sanctioned Rodeo, Jazz and Oysters, and many more events open to peninsula residents as well as tourists. Contact the Long Beach Peninsula Visitors Bureau for more information.

The Peninsula Today

In addition to the special events, there are many permanent features to help explore the peninsula's history. The Discovery Trail follows the footsteps of Captain Clark of the Lewis and Clark expedition as he and his party explored the beach. Near the town of Long Beach, a gray whale skeleton, an obelisk, and a sculpture of a tree representing Clark's pine tree, can be seen along this trail. Clark's tree was sculpted by Stanley Wanless and was transported down the Columbia River to Ilwaco. From there it was moved to its present site, at the end of the Discovery Trail.

The boardwalk at Long Beach runs from Bolstad Avenue to Sid Snyder Drive, providing an opportunity to easily walk from one point to another as it follows along the sand dunes. It is also a place where those with limited mobility or in wheelchairs can get closer to the ocean and sit and watch the waves. Many use the boardwalk as an exercise route; however, no skateboards or bicycles are allowed so it is very safe for walkers. A trail running alongside the boardwalk gives the bicyclist an area to ride and enjoy the same view.

The beach offers many things for tourists and locals to do. Activities include walking along the beach (over 28 miles), beach combing, clamming (during the season), sitting in the sand, and constructing sandcastles. Other activities for all ages are flying kites, picnicking, and surf fishing. Walking on the wet sand is very easy, but walking through the soft sand often offers more of a workout.

Other sites of interest include the mini parks in Long Beach featuring wood sculptures of a seahorse, sea lion, clam, and octopus. The World's Largest Frying Pan is located in one of these parks as well. Also in one park is a sculpture of Lewis and Clark and a tree surrounded by stone markers from different places the Corps of Discovery stopped on their expedition to the Pacific. Planters are placed up and down the main street and are filled with blooming flowers in the spring and summer. Planters are also located on the approach to the ocean and offer a variety of beautiful flowers to be viewed by those who walk by.

Culbertson Park is on Oregon Street in Long Beach. Many softball fields, a tennis court, basketball hoop, playground equipment, and picnic facilities are available there. A skateboard facility is relatively new and adds another activity to the park.

A walking tour of historic Oysterville is another activity many are interested in. A walk through this historic neighborhood shows the architecture of the nineteenth century. Most of the old houses here face the bay. At the historic Oysterville Church is a map of what the town looked like during its heyday.

Even though the area's beaches have long been a draw to tourists, the ocean off the Long Beach Peninsula has always been a dangerous place to swim. Undertows and "sneaker" waves can carry an unaware swimmer out to sea or even drown them. Every year many people become victims of the Pacific Ocean and unfortunately it is often those who have tried to rescue those in trouble who find themselves in a desperate situation.

This Graveyard of the Pacific, even with all the modern safety mechanisms and aids to navigation in place, still lays in wait for the unsuspecting. Boats still run into trouble and get stuck in the sand, break down, or are caught by storms. Shipwrecks can and often do still happen even in this age of technology.

Because of the Japanese Current, which runs along the ocean adjacent to the beach, Japanese fish floats are often found washed ashore. The most coveted of these floats is the glass ball. While many could easily be found in the past, finding one now requires some luck. Beachcombing after a storm often gives an opportunity to be the first to find many kinds of interesting things.

During certain days of the year, the state opens a short clamming season. Hundreds of visitors flock to the beaches to join the locals in the coveted clam digs. In the rain, fog, darkness, or sun, clams are dug. A limit is established, as well as a fee, for a clam license. Visitors should always check with the Washington State Department of Fisheries and Wildlife for dates, limits, and licensing information.

The Long Beach Peninsula has a variety of attractions of interest to all age groups. From a quiet walk on the beach to a noisy Fourth of July fireworks display, many opportunities are available for the tourist and local alike. While an effort has been made to include most of the more popular activities and festivals on the peninsula today, there are many more opportunities to celebrate and take part in activities each year. Check with the Peninsula Visitors Bureau for up-to-date information.

The Long Beach Peninsula has developed over the years through the hard work and innovation of its residents. From the original Chinook settlers to the explorers looking for the mouth of an elusive great river, to the many people who later came to settle in this region, all contributed to the making of the Long Beach Peninsula of today. The rich history of this area speaks of the frustrations and contributions of many different groups of people, who saw in their peninsula a hope for their future. The Long Beach Peninsula of today, like the Long Beach Peninsula of the past, is a place of exploration, a place of beauty, a way of life, and most of all, a home.

NEWS OF THE PENINSULA

The peninsula has had several weekly newspapers during its history: the *Pacific Journal*, the *Ilwaco Advance*, the *North Beach Tribune*, the *Chinook Observer*, and the *Ilwaco Tribune*.

In the *Ilwaco Tribune* in the early part of the twentieth century was a section called "Local and Personal—Items Concerning the Most Prominent, Prominent, and Near Prominent People on the North Beach Peninsula." This section and others held information on who came and went on the peninsula, unusual happenings, and other offbeat information of interest to its readers. Thanks to the *Tribune's* efforts, twenty-first century readers can look back at what was important and interesting to residents and visitors of the time. Some we may see as comical now were taken very serious back then, while others could have been written yesterday. Below are some examples:

> Anderson's horse ran away last Wednesday. It broke the reins and ran through Main St. It nearly hit the axle of a buggy going up hill. It was a terrible runaway. (July 25, 1911)

> The Cape Disappointment Life Saving crew rescued two Oregon fishermen, whose boat had capsized on Peacock Spit Thursday morning and after bringing them to shore went back and brought in their boat and all the fishing gear that could be found. (July 25, 1911)

> J.A. Howerton the telephone man is thinking of running a telephone line to Beards Hollow for the convenience of those who go there late of evening, get lost and have to remain in the woods all night. (August 3, 1911)

THE LONG BEACH PENINSULA

New automobiles are coming to the beach every day and the roads about town are alive with them. In fact, one has to watch closely to be safe. Next year we look for aero planes, when we will not only be kept stepping sideways but nodding and dodging the falling monkey-wrenches, gear-chains and sand ballast as well. (August 3, 1911)

Some of our visitors were around this morning inquiring whether or not the dog caught the cougar? A reporter upon investigation discovered that the report originated with Mr. Kline at the Gilson Hotel, whose peaceful slumbers had been disturbed by a loud mouthed hunting dog that was chasing an old yellow cat around the hotel and making three barks to the jump. (August 10, 1911)

Some miscreant invaded the chicken coop at the home of Widow Wells Saturday night of last week and carried away about two dozen of her young chickens. If there is any thing meaner than stealing chickens from a widow, that crime has not been committed in Ilwaco in a good many years. It is hoped that the thief, or thieves may yet be apprehended and given the very limit of the law. (August 17, 1911)

R. Lovering picked up about 100 fathoms of net on the beach a couple of weeks ago which the owner can recover by paying salvage and eighty cents for this notice. (August 17, 1911)

Ordinance No. 134, entitled "An Ordinance Assessing Two Dollars on Each Male Inhabitant of the Town of Ilwaco for Street Poll Tax" was read and passed on its third reading and ordered published. (March 16, 1912)

Deputy Sheriff Wood took four boys over to Superior Court Wednesday charged with incorrigibility and malicious mischief.

. . . One who has been a boy can sympathize with and pity
wayward boys, one who cannot has never been a boy and is
not much of a man. This drastic action however is sometimes
necessary and should be regarded as a lesson and a warning to
others. (April 27, 1912)

A party of nature fakirs reported to the health department
on Thursday afternoon that a large flock of seagulls had
been observed soaring and circling over the town looking
for something dead. After investigating the matter Dr. Paul
reported that nothing is dead, dying, nor even sick, in Ilwaco
and that the gulls were probably predicting a storm. (September
13, 1913)

If the vandals who bent the top of the wire fence in front of
Jim Vaughn's residence will let themselves be known to him he
will reward them for their trouble. Such contemptible creatures
have no place among human beings. (September 13, 1913)

Will deliver cabbage anywhere on the Peninsula for 2 cents per
pound or sell it at my place for 1 1/2 cents per pound. N.H.
Marks, Cranberry Station. (September 13, 1913)

If you have not paid your dog tax, do it quick. Pay it to Ben
Wise, town treasurer. If the marshal takes your dog you will
have to pay a fine, in addition to the tax, to get your dog back.
We give you this information free of charge, every dog in
the town will pay the tax or there will be no more doggies.
(October 3, 1914)

Ilwaco was treated to an old time runaway last Sunday
afternoon when a team of colts belonging to Jacob Johnson
became frightened and tore madly through the streets until
they came up astride of one of the new electric light poles

when they were brought to a sudden stop. The wagon to which they were hitched was demolished. The team had been brought in from Mr. Johnson's ranch on the Bear River road and the driver left them alone for a moment. What frightened them no one knows. They ran down First Street to Spruce and then out that street until they came to Myrtle Avenue where they left most of the wagon. They swung into this street and soon hit the pole. (February 13, 1922)

Robbers and looters have a special pick at Smith and Smith of Seaview it would seem. Last Monday night their store was entered and all the small change left in the cash register was taken as well as groceries from the shelves. For some days Warner Smith had been sure some one was picking his way into the store by shoving a pin out of a hasp in a sliding door. He tried to catch the culprit and finally padlocked the door. Warner even slept in the store to catch him but on Monday night was called out in his capacity as a constable to make an arrest and thereafter did not return to the store. That night the window was opened and the final robbery committed. Since then the officers have been looking for a young lad who is said to be on parole from the State Training School and has lately taken up his residence in the bushes. (August 22, 1930)

The town of Ilwaco is now the proud possessor of a fire truck designed to enable Chief W.K. Inman and his men to get the hose cart out of the fire hall and to the scene of a fire in short order. It has a brand new coat of paint and when it comes dashing down the street, with siren shrieking, cars are expected to pull for the curb and give the right-of-way. (May 19, 1931)

Appendix

The Ilwaco police department was brought "back to normalcy" by Mayor Brumbach the first of June with the reappointment of W.A. Graham as town cop and water superintendent. Mr. Graham retired some two years ago from this work on account of poor health but is now in good shape for work. This ends the period of brassbound motorcycle police for Ilwaco but it is understood that Oregon is about to establish a "state constabulary" and no doubt there will be use for brass binding, gold braid, and gas carburetors there for the time being. In Ilwaco hereafter the uniform will be overalls, the chief weapon will be a shovel and the motorcycle will be replaced with a pair of stout leather shoes. (June 5, 1931)

BIBLIOGRAPHY

Books

Babcock, Chester D. and Clare Applegate Babcock. *Our Pacific Northwest Yesterday and Today*. San Francisco: Webster Division McGraw-Hill Book Company, 1963.

Davis, Charlotte. *They Remembered*. Book IV. 1994.

Davis, Edgar and Charlotte Davis. *They Remembered*. 1981.

——————. *They Remembered*. Book II. 1983.

Feagans, Raymond. *The Railroad that Ran by the Tide*. Berkeley: Howell North Books, 1972.

Gibbs, James A. *Pacific Graveyard*. Portland: Binford and Mort Publishing, 1993.

Hanft, Marshall. *The Cape Forts: Guardians of the Columbia*. Oregon Historical Society, 1973.

Hussey, John. *Chinook Point and the Story of Fort Columbia*. Washington State Parks and Recreation Commission, 1967.

Kincaid, Trevor. *The Oyster Industry of Willapa Bay, Washington*. Ilwaco, WA: *The Tribune*, 1951.

Lewis, Emanuel R. *Seacoast Fortifications of the United States*. Annapolis: Naval Institute Press, 1993.

McDonald, Lucile. *Coast Country: A History of Southwest Washington*. Long Beach, WA: Midway Printing, 1989.

Moulton, Gary E., ed. *The Definitive Journals of Lewis and Clark: Down the Columbia to Fort Clatsop*. Volume 6 (November 2, 1805–March 22, 1806) Nebraska Edition. Lincoln, NE: University of Nebraska Press, 1990.

Pacific Coast Cranberries. Long Beach, WA: Pacific Coast Cranberry Research Foundation, 1997.

Smith, Courtland L. *Salmon Fishers of the Columbia*. Corvallis, OR: Oregon State University Press, 1979.

South Bend Journal. Pacific County Edition. South Bend, WA: 1900.

Thoreau, Henry David. *Cape Cod 1817–1862.* Princeton: Princeton University Press, 1988.

Williams, L.R. *Our Pacific County.* Raymond, WA: *The Raymond Herald*, 1930.

——————. *Chinook by the Sea.* Portland: Kilman Stationery and Printing Company, 1924.

Newspapers

The *North Beach Tribune*
The *Ilwaco Tribune*
The *Tribune*
The *Chinook Observer*

INDEX

Index